QUICK WIN DIGITAL MARKETING

Answers to your top 100 digital marketing questions

Annmarie Hanlon & Joanna Akins

Published by
OAK TREE PRESS
19 Rutland Street, Cork, Ireland
www.oaktreepress.com

© 2009 Annmarie Hanlon and Joanna Akins

A catalogue record of this book is
available from the British Library.

ISBN 978 1 904887 87 4

INTRODUCTION

QUICK WIN DIGITAL MARKETING is aimed at marketers, entrepreneurs and business managers who want to understand and use digital marketing. This book is designed so you can dip in and out seeking answers to questions as they arise.

There are five sections to the book:

- **Digital Essentials:** An introduction to digital marketing techniques and tools (Twitter, Facebook, LinkedIn, etc) and how your business can use them.

- **Digital Toolbox:** Practical advice on how to do specific things using digital applications.

- **Digital Marketing:** How you can use digital marketing techniques and tools to promote your business / products / services.

- **Branding Online:** A critical topic for businesses of all sizes.

- **Managing, Measuring and Making Money Online:** Where it all comes together.

In addition, using the grid in the **Contents**, you can search for questions and answers across a range of topics, including:

- Blogs / microblogs.
- Email.
- Mobile.
- Photo / audio / video.
- Social media.
- Surveys.
- Web.

Finally, an **Appendix** gives the URLs of the many websites referenced throughout the book.

Enjoy the book, spread the word and get connected – we wish you lots of quick wins and success in your digital marketing!

Annmarie Hanlon and Joanna Akins

September 2009

CONTENTS

DIGITAL ESSENTIALS

	Blogs / microblogs	Email	Mobile	Photo / audio / video	Social media	Surveys	Web	PAGE
Q1 Where do we start with digital marketing?	✓	✓	✓	✓	✓	✓	✓	2
Q2 What are the advantages and disadvantages of digital marketing?	✓	✓	✓	✓	✓	✓	✓	4
Q3 What is search engine optimisation?							✓	6
Q4 What is search engine marketing?							✓	8
Q5 What is social networking?	✓		✓	✓	✓			9
Q6 What is viral marketing?	✓	✓	✓	✓	✓		✓	14
Q7 What is Twitter?	✓		✓		✓		✓	16
Q8 What can Twitter do for our business?	✓		✓		✓		✓	19
Q9 How can we use Twitter to market our business / products / services?	✓		✓		✓		✓	21
Q10 How can we use Twitter for market research?	✓		✓		✓	✓	✓	23
Q11 What is Facebook?	✓		✓	✓	✓		✓	25
Q12 What are Facebook fans and why do we need them?	✓		✓	✓	✓		✓	28
Q13 What can Facebook do for our business?	✓		✓	✓	✓	✓	✓	29

DIGITAL ESSENTIALS

	Blogs / microblogs	Email	Mobile	Photo / audio / video	Social media	Surveys	Web	PAGE
Q14 How can we use Facebook to market our business / products / services?	☑		☑	☑	☑		☑	30
Q15 How can we use Facebook for market research?	☑		☑	☑	☑	☑	☑	32
Q16 What is LinkedIn?					☑		☑	34
Q17 How can we use LinkedIn to market our business / products / services?					☑		☑	36
Q18 How can we use LinkedIn for market research?					☑	☑	☑	38
Q19 What is Ecademy?					☑		☑	40
Q20 How can we use Ecademy to market our business / products / services?					☑		☑	41
Q21 What is Second Life?					☑		☑	43
Q22 What can Second Life do for our business?					☑		☑	44
Q23 What is YouTube?			☑	☑	☑		☑	46
Q24 What can YouTube do for our business?			☑	☑	☑		☑	47
Q25 What are social bookmarking sites?					☑		☑	49

DIGITAL ESSENTIALS

	Blogs / microblogs	Email	Mobile	Photo / audio / video	Social media	Surveys	Web	PAGE
Q26 What is blogging and how do we start?	☑		☑	☑	☑		☑	51
Q27 How do we use blogging to market our business / products / services?	☑		☑	☑	☑		☑	53
Q28 What is podcasting and how can we use it in our business?	☑		☑	☑	☑		☑	55
Q29 What are landing pages and how do we use them?							☑	56
Q30 What are content management systems and how do we use them?							☑	58
Q31 What is mobile marketing and how can we use it to market our business / products / services?			☑					60
Q32 Why are search engine rankings important?							☑	62
Q33 What are the basic rules of web usability?							☑	64

DIGITAL TOOLBOX

	Blogs / microblogs	Email	Mobile	Photo / audio / video	Social media	Surveys	Web	PAGE
Q34 How can we build websites ourselves without using a web designer?							☑	68
Q35 What contact information must appear as a minimum on our website / blog?	☑						☑	70
Q36 What are we required to do to protect the privacy of visitors to our website / blog?	☑						☑	72
Q37 Where can we get stock photos for our website / blog?	☑			☑			☑	74
Q38 How do we build links to / from other websites?	☑						☑	76
Q39 How do we find and get followers on Twitter?	☑		☑		☑		☑	78
Q40 How do we get more content for our blog?	☑				☑		☑	80
Q41 How do we buy a domain name and which domain extensions should we buy?							☑	82
Q42 How do we select a web designer?							☑	85
Q43 How do we brief a web designer?							☑	87
Q44 How do we get higher / better search rankings?							☑	89

DIGITAL TOOLBOX	Blogs / microblogs	Email	Mobile	Photo / audio / video	Social media	Surveys	Web	PAGE
Q45 How do we choose keywords or keyphrases for our website / blog?	☑						☑	91
Q46 How do we create a social networking policy?					☑			93
Q47 How do we use LinkedIn to drive traffic to our website?					☑		☑	95
Q48 How do we make connections on LinkedIn with people we don't know?					☑		☑	96
Q49 What are 'tagging' and 'retweets' on Twitter and how do we use them?	☑		☑		☑		☑	98
Q50 How do we verify our Twitter account?	☑		☑		☑		☑	99
Q51 How do we register our Facebook page?	☑		☑		☑		☑	100
Q52 How can we post our own videos onto our website / blog?				☑	☑		☑	101
Q53 Where can we post press releases online?							☑	103

DIGITAL MARKETING	Blogs / microblogs	Email	Mobile	Photo / audio / video	Social media	Surveys	Web	PAGE
Q54 How do we start a digital marketing campaign?	☑	☑	☑	☑	☑	☑	☑	106
Q55 How can we use digital applications / tools / techniques to stay in touch online with our customers?	☑	☑	☑	☑	☑	☑	☑	108
Q56 How can we interact with our customers online?	☑	☑	☑	☑	☑	☑	☑	110
Q57 How do we identify our customers using digital communications?	☑	☑	☑	☑	☑	☑	☑	112
Q58 Should we include attachments in email campaigns?		☑						114
Q59 Can we send an enewsletter to everyone on our database?		☑					☑	116
Q60 What rules apply to contacting people online?		☑			☑		☑	118
Q61 How do we create an enewsletter / ezine?		☑					☑	119
Q62 Where can we find subscribers to send an enewsletter to?	☑	☑			☑		☑	121
Q63 How often should we make contact with our customers online?		☑					☑	123
Q64 How can we gather feedback from customers on new products / services?	☑				☑	☑	☑	125

DIGITAL MARKETING

	Blogs / microblogs	Email	Mobile	Photo / audio / video	Social media	Surveys	Web	PAGE
Q65 How can we use SMS to contact customers / potential customers?			☑			☑		127
Q66 How do we run webinars for existing / potential customers?							☑	129
Q67 How can our team collaborate online?	☑				☑		☑	131
Q68 How do we prevent our online marketing being seen as spam?	☑	☑	☑		☑		☑	133
Q69 How do we make our online marketing interesting to customers / potential customers?	☑	☑	☑	☑	☑		☑	134
Q70 How can we use customer surveys online?						☑		136
Q71 How do we get our blog posts to a wider audience?	☑							138
Q72 How do we get all our staff involved in digital marketing?	☑	☑	☑	☑	☑	☑	☑	140
Q73 How can we work with our fans on Facebook?	☑		☑		☑		☑	142
Q74 How can we harness our followers on Twitter?	☑		☑		☑		☑	144
Q75 How do we advertise online?							☑	146
Q76 Should we handle our own PR online or engage an agency?	☑	☑	☑		☑		☑	149
Q77 How do we select an agency to handle our PR online?	☑	☑	☑		☑		☑	151

BRANDING ONLINE	Blogs / microblogs	Email	Mobile	Photo / audio / video	Social media	Surveys	Web	PAGE
Q78 How is branding online different?	☑	☑	☑		☑		☑	154
Q79 How do we prevent brand damage if our employees use social networking sites?					☑			156
Q80 How can we add credibility to our online presence?	☑	☑	☑		☑		☑	158
Q81 What should we include in an online profile?					☑			160
Q82 How can we brand our business on social media sites?					☑			161

MANAGING, MEASURING AND MAKING MONEY ONLINE	Blogs / microblogs	Email	Mobile	Photo / audio / video	Social media	Surveys	Web	PAGE
Q83 How do we manage Twitter and Facebook?	☑		☑		☑			164
Q84 How can we publish to several sites at the same time?	☑		☑		☑			166
Q85 How do we tweet when we're busy and manage multiple Twitter accounts?	☑		☑		☑			167
Q86 What free software can we use to help manage Twitter?	☑		☑		☑			169
Q87 How can we manage blog posts?	☑		☑		☑			171
Q88 How can we monitor and measure online traffic?							☑	172
Q89 How can we use Google Analytics to measure our web traffic?							☑	174
Q90 How many visitors to our website do we need to make one sale?							☑	175
Q91 How can we test our email campaigns?		☑						177
Q92 How can we monitor our brand or company online?	☑	☑	☑		☑		☑	179
Q93 How can we trust what we read online?							☑	181
Q94 How can charities use Facebook to generate income?	☑		☑		☑			183

MANAGING, MEASURING AND MAKING MONEY ONLINE	Blogs / microblogs	Email	Mobile	Photo / audio / video	Social media	Surveys	Web	PAGE
Q95 How can Twitter generate sales for our business?	☑		☑		☑			185
Q96 How can we set up affiliate marketing programmes?							☑	187
Q97 How can we monetise Second Life?					☑			189
Q98 How do we set up a PayPal business account?							☑	191
Q99 How can we make money on our website / blog?	☑						☑	193
Q100 What are the top 10 tips for successful digital marketing?	☑	☑	☑	☑	☑	☑	☑	194

DIGITAL ESSENTIALS

Think of yourself as on the threshold of unparalleled success. A whole, clear, glorious life lies before you. Achieve! Achieve!
Andrew Carnegie

Q1   Where do we start with digital marketing?

Marketing is about understanding and meeting your clients' needs profitably. Digital marketing, which is also known as internet marketing, i-marketing, web marketing, online marketing, or emarketing, is about marketing products or services over the Internet or via mobile technology.

Digital marketing techniques include search engine marketing (SEM), search engine optimisation (SEO), email marketing, viral marketing, blogging, microblogging, podcasting, vodcasting, photo and video sharing, social networking, virtual worlds and mobile phone campaigns using SMS.

Digital marketing tools include applications such as:

- **WordPress** and **Blogger** (blogging).
- **Twitter** (microblogging).
- **Facebook** and **LinkedIn** (social networking).
- **Second Life** (virtual worlds).
- **Flickr** and **YouTube** (photo and video sharing).
- **Google Analytics** (monitoring results).

Seven years ago, when we asked businesspeople, "Do you have a company website?", not everyone could say "Yes". Today, to be without a website provokes a reaction of disbelief. To be in business, you *need* a web presence. We believe that, within the next five years, companies will adopt digital marketing in the same way. The key issue is getting started.

You must decide:

- How does digital marketing fit within your overall marketing plan / budget?
- What do you want to achieve through digital marketing?

- Who do you want to talk to?
- How much time can you allocate?
- Who in your company can manage and monitor this activity?
- What's the likely payback – and when?

Digital marketing enables small businesses to compete with bigger businesses, as any company of any size can gain instant – and usually free – access to a range of digital marketing tools online.

But there's a learning curve in understanding the mechanics of the various techniques and tools – and a payback curve in seeing tangible financial benefit for your business. Nonetheless, the increasing number of stories of business being won or sales being made through Twitter, Facebook or other tools means that you cannot afford to ignore digital marketing.

Start by dipping your toe in the water through Twitter or, if you have more time, go for a blog. Better still, combine the two (we assume you already have a website!).

See also

Q3   What is search engine optimisation?
Q4   What is search engine marketing?
Q5   What is social networking?
Q6   What is viral marketing?
Q7   What is Twitter?
Q11   What is Facebook?
Q16   What is LinkedIn?
Q21   What is Second Life?
Q23   What is YouTube?
Q26   What is blogging and how do we start?
Q28   What is podcasting and how can we use it in our business?
Q31   What is mobile marketing and how can we use it to market our business / products / services?
Q88   How can we monitor and measure online traffic?
Q99   How can we make money on our website / blog?

Q2   What are the advantages and disadvantages of digital marketing?

Digital marketing provides businesses with the opportunity to communicate with a vast, global, audience at a low – usually, free – entry cost.

The advantages of digital marketing include:

- It is comparatively inexpensive for the target audience numbers involved.
- You can create instant campaigns to address hot topics.
- You can try different forms of advertising and assess the results.
- You can display videos demonstrating the product or service.
- It can be highly personalised (ads on specific websites, SMS direct to the individual's desk, handbag or pocket).
- You can show feedback from happy customers (great opportunities for hotels / accommodation with review websites, such as **TripAdvisor** – but you can add a feedback section on your own website).
- You can measure and monitor responses to ad campaigns at the click of a mouse.
- You can see exactly how many people opened an enewsletter and when, and what further action (if any) they took.

The disadvantages of digital marketing include:

- There can be many legal issues to consider, as compliance varies according to your location and the technique used – from ads on **Facebook** to emailshots.
- Delivery of emailshots can be blocked or registered as spam.
- It can be wasted on customers with limited or no internet connectivity.

- There is still no ability to touch or smell products online.
- You are dependent on your customers' technology; their computer and internet connections are outside your control.

However, the greatest challenge is the willingness (or otherwise!) of senior managers to adopt digital marketing.

See also
Q1   Where do we start with digital marketing?
Q35   What contact information must appear as a minimum on our website / blog?
Q36   What are we required to do to protect the privacy of visitors to our website / blog?
Q60   What rules apply to contacting people online?
Q68   How do we prevent our online marketing being seen as spam?
Q88   How can we monitor and measure online traffic?

Q3   What is search engine optimisation?

Search engines, such as **Google** and **Bing**, use mathematical algorithms or formulae to analyse a user's question or search query in order to provide web pages that attempt to most closely answer the question or relate to the search term.

Search engine optimisation (SEO) ensures that your website is constructed in such a way that your webpages are returned first (or on the first results page) for any relevant search, since most users rarely look much beyond the first page of search results.

SEO seeks to understand the search engines' algorithms (which change constantly) and to meet their criteria. In this way, an optimised website achieves 'naturally high' search responses and therefore has less need for paid advertising to bring traffic to it. For example, the **HomeSwapper** website contains relevant links and, as a result, generates high search results ranking and thus significant traffic.

Unless your website is regularly listed within the first page of search results for relevant search terms / keywords, its search engine 'ranking' probably needs to be improved. Follow the guidelines in the checklist on the next page.

You will also find guidance from the search engines at the sites below:

- **Google Webmaster tools**:
  http://www.google.com/webmasters/checklist.
- **Search Engine Optimization Made Easy**:
  http://www.seome.org.
- **Bing Webmaster Tools**:
  http://www.bing.com/toolbox/webmasters.

You need to be able to answer "Yes" to these questions:

Checklist	Y/N
Has your website been submitted to Google, **MSN** / Bing and **Yahoo**?	
Has your web developer excluded 'Flash' or 'frames' from the website design?	
Does your website contain a site map?	
Does each page contain key phrases likely to be used by searchers?	
Does your website contain relevant links to and from your site?	
Do you monitor your website and where it appears in search engine results?	

If you decide to use a SEO consultant:

- Ask for references from his / her previous clients and check them out.

- Recognise that you will need to commit to working with them for six to 12 months, as SEO takes time.

- Agree a budget and target results before you start.

See also
Q4   What is search engine marketing?
Q32   Why are search engine rankings so important?
Q44   How do we get higher / better search engine rankings?
Q89   How can we use Google Analytics to measure our web traffic?

Q4   What is search engine marketing?

Search engine marketing (SEM) is also known as search engine advertising.

On sites like **Google AdWords** and **Microsoft AdCenter**, you bid for your preferred keywords against other advertisers. When these words appear in users' search queries, your ad appears alongside the search results – usually labelled as 'sponsored links' or 'sponsored results'.

Most SEM is on a 'pay per click' (PPC) basis, under which you only pay when a user clicks through from an ad to your website. Thus SEM is very cost-effective, since the ad is only triggered by relevant search terms and you only pay for actual traffic delivered to your site.

Google Adwords and Microsoft AdCenter both provide some online advice in choosing keywords and managing SEM campaigns.

Just as for SEO, if you decide to use a SEM consultant:

- Ask for references from his / her previous clients and check them out.

- Recognise that you will need to commit to working with them for several months.

- Agree a budget and target results before you start.

See also
Q3   What is search engine optimisation?
Q75   How do we advertise online?

Q5   What is social networking?

Social networking provides a way to connect people of similar interests, regardless of geography, on a website. A wide range of social networking sites provide networking tools for individuals (both personally and professionally) and for businesses, depending on the site, as well as offering a platform for friends and family to keep up with each other. Some of the most important sites are:

Site	User profile	Users (and source)
Bebo	Mainly personal rather than business-to-business. Described as 'MySpace meets Facebook, with video-sharing and built-in Skype'.	40 million (Bebo, via www.web-strategist.com, November 2008).
Ecademy	For businesspeople who connect online on the website and offline at events and meetings.	500,000 unique users per month (Ecademy, August 2009).
eHow	Online community that allows visitors to research, share, and discuss instructional solutions that help complete day-to-day tasks and projects.	23 million unique visitors (comScore, July 2009); over 45 million (internal data, www.demandmedia.com).

Site	User profile	Users (and source)
Facebook	Mainly personal rather than business-to-business but increasing number of businesses creating 'pages' for branding. Less than one-third students; fastest growing demographic is 35 years+.	250 million (Facebook, August 2009); 276 million (comScore, March 2009).
Flickr	Online photo management and sharing application.	2 million images and 26 million unique visitors (Compete.com, July 2009).
Hi5	One of the largest social entertainment web sites. 43% users aged 15 to 24.	80 million registered accounts and c.46 million unique users per month (Hi5, August 2009).
LinkedIn	Business-to-business focus, aimed at professionals. Represents 170 industries and 200 countries.	45 million (LinkedIn, August 2009).

Site	User profile	Users (and source)
MySpace	Mainly personal rather than business-to-business. 30% aged 15 to 24.	200 million (comScore, March 2009).
Plaxo Pulse	Online address book with social networking.	40 million (Plaxo, August 2009).
Plurk	Similar to Twitter, a free social networking and micro-blogging service that allows users to send updates (called 'plurks') through short messages or links, up to 140 characters.	Not known – c.250,000 unique visitors (Compete.com, February 2009).

Site	User profile	Users (and source)
SlideShare	Allows uploading and sharing of PowerPoint presentations, Word documents and Adobe PDFs. Users are highly-educated (62% college degree; 19% Masters or PhD); affluent (25%+ earn $100K+/year); adult (64% 35 years+ and 32% 18 to 34).	17 million unique visitors (SlideShare, August 2009).
Twitter	A mix of personal and business-to-business. Micro-blogging allows users to send updates (called 'tweets') through short messages or links, up to 140 characters.	44.5 million unique visitors (http://www.businessinsider.com/chart-of-the-day-twitters-boom-around-the-world-2009-8).
Xing.com	Alternative to LinkedIn in Germany; English version available.	8 million (Xing, August 2009).

Site	User profile	Users (and source)
YouTube	Video-sharing website. User base is broad in age range, 18 to 55, evenly divided between males and females, spanning all geographies.	71 million unique users per month (YouTube, August 2009).

HINT

Not all social networks are suitable for all businesses. You need to decide which networks match your business's needs and start exploring.

See also
Q6   What is viral marketing?
Q7   What is Twitter?
Q11 What is Facebook?
Q16 What is LinkedIn?
Q19 What is Ecademy?
Q23 What is YouTube?
Q46 How do we create a social networking policy?
Q79 How do we prevent brand damage if our employees use social networking sites?
Q82 How can we brand our business on social media sites?

Q6 What is viral marketing?

Viral marketing is a newer marketing technique that encourages recipients to pass on information – and so, like a virus, the message spreads.

Viral marketing involves creating emails, videos, podcasts, photos or slideshows, which you then share among your friends and add to social media sharing sites (such as **YouTube** and **Facebook**). For viral marketing to be successful, you need to encourage the receiver to send your message on to their friends or colleagues. This means that the message or information needs to be:

- Interesting or amusing.
- Creative or different.
- Special or secret.

The reason viral marketing has become successful is due to ease of use. Once the message has been created, it can be passed from one person to another simply by someone hitting the 'forward' button. Distribution of the message is free and can capture a worldwide audience within hours.

Successful viral marketing campaigns include:

- Free software such as **Hotmail.com**, which provides free email accounts that include advertising messages in the emails. Every time a user sends an email, they're spreading the word for Hotmail.

- Ads or videos promoting a brand, such as the Touch of Gold video featuring the footballer Ronaldinho training in his Nike footwear.

- Smaller companies like **Blendtec**, which re-launched its food blender by videoing its chief executive blending everyday items (including an iPhone!) and then adding the video to YouTube.

- Social media websites such as Facebook, **MySpace** and **LinkedIn** that encourage you to get your friends and colleagues to join.

See also

Q5   What is social networking?
Q11   What is Facebook?
Q16   What is LinkedIn?
Q23   What is YouTube?

Q7   What is Twitter?

Twitter is about answering the question, "What are you doing?", in less than 140 characters, via texting, instant message, or the web. (To put this in context, that first sentence above is 135 characters.) A message on Twitter is known as a 'tweet' and people adding messages are said to be 'tweeting'.

Twitter started in 2006 and gained momentum in 2009 when Oprah Winfrey started tweeting. Popular with celebrities and politicians, Twitter is now being used by journalists, big brands, local councils, sports clubs and smaller businesses, as well as individuals in all walks of life. Increasingly, Twitter is being used by businesses worldwide to communicate with customers, potential customers and influencers.

In July 2009, the *New York Times* reported that Curtis Kimball, a street vendor selling crème brûlées in San Francisco, had noticed someone new in the queue. When he asked how the customer had heard about the food cart, the answer was "he had read about it on Twitter". Now Kimball tweets daily, letting customers know where to find him.

Communicating with so few words means that you need to be succinct. It also means that a form of Twitter shorthand has developed – for example:

- **@username + message:** This directs a tweet at another person which can be seen by their followers: @annmariehanlon we're attending the SME show in Dublin.

- **D username + message:** A D or DM sends a person a direct and private message. No one else can see a DM or Direct Message: D joannaakins Brian running late, delays in Cork.

- **WHOIS username:** Type a whois request into your Twitter box and it shows the short biography of the person, as long as their updates are not private: whois joannaakins. (Twitter only lets you see this info for a few seconds!)

- **GET username:** This retrieves the latest Twitter update posted by the person but, if they have not tweeted for a while, it can take sometime: get brianokane.

- **#hashtag:** These are used to #tag tweets to make it easier for people searching on Twitter. They are the equivalent of Twitter keywords: #followfriday to see who people have started following.

- **RT – retweet:** These are like forwarding an email to all your followers. To credit the original tweeter, add "RT" plus the originator's username at the beginning of the tweet: RT @annmariehanlon this is a retweet example.

The power of Twitter is that, although it is a web-based application, you can tweet from many mobile phones using applications such as **Twitterfon**. Wherever you are, whatever your experience, whenever it happens, you can share it with the world. You can give instant feedback on customer service, share information about airport delays, political changes, even the weather and you can get real-time opinions about places or events.

Twitter is free of charge, but does require some time to get to grips with. You need to:

- Decide how you can best use Twitter (to raise your profile, engage customers, gain feedback, promote new products).
- Create a Twitter account.
- Start tweeting.
- Gain followers and follow other people.

HINT

If you're struggling to stay within 140 characters, there are tools to help you shorten your comments or weblinks, such as TinyURL, ShortURL, Bit.ly, Ow.ly or Tweetdeck.com.

See also

Q8 What can Twitter do for our business?

Many people do not understand **Twitter** initially – they just 'don't get it'. Frequent questions and comments include "What is the point?" and "It's such a waste of time". But one of the fastest-growing business segments online is creating applications to make Twitter more useful for companies.

Today, Twitter adds value to businesses in the following ways:

- Comments on Twitter are indexed by **Google** within hours, improving your search profile.
- Your tweets can drive traffic to your website.
- Twitter gives you direct contact with journalists and editors.
- Company news can be seen by journalists and potential customers as it happens.
- You have contact with people who may not normally take your phonecall.
- Promotional messages can be promoted to a wider audience than your existing customers, with the explicit endorsement of those who retweet them.
- Twitter raises your company's online profile.

In addition, using Twitter you can:

- Promote time-limited offers – the last few seats for a movie starting in 30 minutes time, for example.
- Create and organise events online and 'tweetups' offline – using **Twtvite**.
- Make coupons for special offers for Twitter customers – using **Twtqpon**.
- Post jobs and get applications online via Twitter – on **Twtjobs**.
- Provide customer service and gain feedback from customers on products or services.

- Test and promote new products.

- Build mailing lists.

- Piggy-back on current events and provide a relevant offer – for example, forehead thermometers to check for swine flu.

- Create a Twitter business card – **Twtbizcard**.

- Have conversations with customers.

- Monitor your brand.

| HINT | Don't forget that whatever tweets you add to Twitter will be there forever. Be careful about making any angry outbursts about other people or companies, as Twitter allows users to search on both positive and negative comments. |

See also

Q9 How can we use Twitter to market our business / products / services?

Using **Twitter**, or any online tool, should be part of a wider marketing plan. Rather than considering a specific tool in isolation, think about your objectives and what your company is trying to achieve.

For example, your business may wish to:

- Find new customers.
- Make friends / contacts with journalists.
- Provide 'followers' with special offers.
- Build a larger mailing list.
- Drive traffic to your website or blog.
- Share photos, video clips or podcasts with a wider audience.
- Promote new products or services.
- Manage customer services.
- Recruit staff.

Once you have decided what you want to achieve, you can decide your approach.

Good business tweets need to be informative, useful and / or good enough to share. You can tweet about:

- New products or services (not hard sell).
- New blog posts.
- Asking or answering a question.
- Facts and figures.
- Local breaking news.
- Information that may be of interest to your customers / followers.

- Your availability to meet people at exhibitions, conferences or other public meetings.

In addition, you can repeat someone else's tweet (re-tweet).

The best way to manage Twitter is to allocate 10 minutes at the start of your day to update what you are doing. Note that if you open a Twitter account and don't use it, Twitter will close it.

 If you add a web link to your website into a tweet, consider organising a dedicated landing page for the link so that you can measure the traffic from Twitter.

See also

Q7   What is Twitter?

Q27   How do we use blogging to market our business / products / services?

Q29   What are landing pages and how do we use them?

Q64   How can we gather feedback from customers on new products / services?

Q74   How can we harness our followers on Twitter?

Q95   How can Twitter generate sales for our business?

Q10 How can we use Twitter for market research?

The latest trends or topics are discussed on **Twitter**, as it captures breaking news, up-to-the-minute themes and most recent ideas from people all over the world.

You can use Twitter to:

- Research your own company.
- Find out what people think about your competitors.
- Ask questions of your followers and others – **Polldaddy for Twitter**.
- Add polls to your website, Twitter or **Facebook** page – **Twtpoll**.
- Find customers in your areas – **NearbyTweets**.
- Find groups that may be relevant to your business – **Twibes**.
- See which groups your followers have joined – **Twitree**.
- Find businesses, entrepreneurs and investors on Twitter – **TwtBiz**.

Searches on Twitter may bring up hundreds of responses. To narrow your search, you can use the following shorthand:

Tool	Example	Will only provide results
" "	"marketing plan"	Containing the exact phrase "marketing plan".
#	#marketing	Containing the hashtag #marketing.
from:	from:brianokane	Of tweets sent from Brian O'Kane.
to:	to:annmariehanlon	Of tweets sent to Annmarie Hanlon.
near:	"coffee shop" near: "Cork"	Containing your search term: coffee shop, near Cork.

Tool	Example	Will only provide results
OR	london OR dublin	Containing the words London or Dublin or both.
-	ireland - dublin	Containing the word Ireland but *not* Dublin.
:)	Coffee :)	Containing the word coffee and with a positive attitude.
:(	Coffee :(	Containing the word coffee and with a negative attitude.

HINT

If you are conducting research and need answers from a larger pool of people, ask followers to retweet (RT) to get more potential responders to your questions: 'Do you prefer customer service online or by telephone? Pls RT!'.

Other useful Twitter-related websites include: **Hashtags**, which shows the latest Twitter topics; **Tweetzi**, a Twitter search engine; **Twitscoop** or **Twitturly**, for latest trends on Twitter; and **Twitterment**, a Twitter search engine.

See also
Q7   What is Twitter?
Q15   How can we use Facebook for market research?
Q18   How can we use LinkedIn for market research?
Q64   How can we gather feedback from customers on new products / services?
Q70   How can we use customer surveys online?

Q11   What is Facebook?

Facebook is a social networking website that allows people to stay in touch with friends and family, current and past colleagues, post photos online, share and organise events. Started by college students in the US in 2004, Facebook now claims over 250 million members worldwide – almost as many as the population of the USA, making it (if it were a country) the 4th largest country in the world.

Membership of Facebook is free but you need to register and create a user name and password. This creates your personal Facebook 'profile'.

If you plan to use Facebook for your business, you should select a business account, which gives you the ability to create a Facebook 'page'. Pages are designed for businesses only, to share information, to interact with customers / fans and to create a brand presence on Facebook.

Facebook features include:

Feature	What this does
Wall	The key area to share information about your profile and for adding new things, like photos, videos and notes.
Links	Allows you to add links to other websites, podcasts, etc.
Photos	Here you can add and see photos, which may include 'tags' with notes about who is in the photo and what they're doing.
Newsfeed	This is a personalised information update, which can show updates from your Wall, links and photos, as well as shared comments between friends and information about forthcoming events such as a friend's birthday.

Facebook is being used successfully by many groups and associations to promote their causes and to recruit new supporters. The **Bat**

Conservation Trust, for example, uses Facebook as a tool to keep supporters informed, share details of events and encourage fans to donate online. Charities and people seeking sponsorship can add a charity payment site, such as **JustGiving.com** or **theBigGive**, into their Facebook pages to monitor how much money has been raised.

Using Facebook pages, businesses can:

- Create content for Facebook users.

- Add photos of products.

- Provide special offers.

Customers or non-customers can become 'fans' and they can display information about your business on their Wall, receive your updates and start engaging in conversations. Additionally, their friends can see your information and could also become fans. Facebook claims that more than 3 million users become fans of Facebook pages every day.

Facebook now offers usernames for Facebook pages, which means companies can have a personalised URL for their page – for example, the Evonomie Facebook page URL is www.facebook.com/evonomie. To qualify for this format (as opposed to the standard www.facebook.com/pages/Evonomie/22321854878), a page must have a minimum number of fans (currently, 25 for newly-created pages).

If you want to share an event on Facebook, you can create a 'group'.

One of the reasons that Facebook's popularity continues to grow is its availability on mobile phones like the iPhone. There's a downside to its popularity, though – many businesses have become unhappy about the amount of time their staff are spending on Facebook during the working day, which emphasises the need for a 'social networking policy'.

See also

Q12   What are Facebook fans and why do we need them?

A **Facebook** fan is someone who has found a business or brand page that interests them and has clicked on the 'become a fan' button. Fans are your Facebook database. They can be sent 'updates' about new products, special offers and latest news.

When someone joins your page as a fan, this information is published in their News Feed, which all their friends can see, thus spreading the word about your company or brand. The more fans you have, the greater the profile you get.

In addition, if you have more than 25 fans, Facebook will change your page's URL to http://www.facebook.com/yourbusinessname, which makes it easier to find.

Pages are useful because:

- They are public and can be found via search engines. Most of Facebook is hidden behind a login, but pages are available to everyone.

- Links can be added, which can drive traffic to your blog, website or other online presence, creating further opportunities for viral marketing.

However, it requires work to build your database of fans. Your **Twitter** followers are a good starting point, especially if they retweet your appeal for Facebook fans to their followers.

See also
Q73   How can we work with our fans on Facebook?

Q13   What can Facebook do for our business?

Facebook can be used for:

- Creating brand awareness.
- Gaining reviews from happy customers.
- Defusing feedback from unhappy customers.
- Conducting research.
- Testing products and services.
- Recruiting staff.

Businesses can use Facebook to stay in touch with former staff, to share plans and ideas and to run recruitment drives. Brands can carry out research with their 'fans'. You can use Facebook as a trial or test centre, getting feedback on new ideas and providing early access (sneak peeks) to new advertising campaigns and special offers.

Depending on your audience, a Facebook campaign may make more commercial sense than other advertising options: Gap clothing has dropped TV ads in favour of a dedicated campaign on Facebook (InsideFacebook.com, 19 August 2009). Facebook provides guidance online on how to set up a Facebook advertising campaign.

> **HINT**   Be aware that any posts you make on your company page on Facebook also appear in your personal profile!

See also
Q79   How do we prevent brand damage if our employees use social networking sites?
Q82   How can we brand our business on social media sites?
Q94   How can charities use Facebook to generate income?

Q14   How can we use Facebook to market our business / products / services?

With over 250 million members worldwide, **Facebook** provides opportunities to communicate with many different groups of people.

There are two options for businesses:

- To create a page and generate fans through other fans, by using viral marketing.
- To create a page and use **Facebook Ads**.

Generating fans through viral marketing requires time and effort to add interesting content, such as podcasts, **YouTube** videos, or special offers, which existing fans will share with their friends.

Facebook gathers lots of personal information about its users and uses this to allow businesses to target advertising to specific users by:

- Location.
- Age (by default, Facebook targets only users aged 18 and older).
- Birthday.
- Gender.
- Keywords.
- Education.
- Company, organisation or other workplace.
- Relationship status.
- With certain interests.

Options for advertising on Facebook are 'pay per click' (also known as 'cost per click' or CPC) or 'pay for views' (known as 'cost per mille', 'cost per thousand impressions' or CPM). You can set maximum bids and daily limits.

Advertising on Facebook is controversial, as many users are unhappy at being targeted based on their personal information, especially when that information is used to create ads on their friends' profiles. In July 2009, Facebook stated it *"occasionally pairs advertisements with relevant social actions from a user's friends to create Facebook Ads. Facebook Ads make advertisements more interesting and more tailored to you and your friends. These respect all privacy rules. You may opt out of appearing in your friends' Facebook Ads below"*. However, this was interpreted by users as *"Facebook agreed to let third party advertisers use your posted photos WITHOUT your permission"*. The controversy reflects the tension between users' desire for free social networking and the site-owners' desire to monetise the community they have created.

If you are selling products to consumers, Facebook can help to raise your brand profile, to drive traffic to a sales website and potentially to generate new customers. If you are selling business to business, consider **LinkedIn** instead.

See also

Q15 How can we use Facebook for market research?

Developers have created **Facebook** applications (apps), mostly free, that allow businesses to conduct surveys, votes, polls and quizzes. Facebook also provides polls to get quick answers to simple questions.

Evonomie Polls	Result
1 poll	View Poll	Delete	Edit	Invite Friends To Vote

Do you use Twitter?
3 votes

Do you use Twitter?

Yes	33%
No	67%

To start a Facebook poll, you:

- Log into Facebook.
- Click on Facebook Applications, search for 'poll' and decide which application you prefer.
- Add your chosen application to your page.
- Edit your page and open the poll application.
- Type a simple question.
- Return to your page and publish the poll.

HINT

If you create multiple polls for a page, only the most recent one will be on display.

See also
Q10 How can we use Twitter for market research?
Q18 How can we use LinkedIn for market research?

Q64 How can we gather feedback from customers on new products / services?

Q70 How can we use customer surveys online?

Q16   What is LinkedIn?

LinkedIn is an online social network, whose aim is to connect professionals locally, nationally and internationally. Today, LinkedIn claims 45 million members from over 200 countries.

Basic membership is free and allows you to:

* Create a profile about your work, qualifications and experience.

* Demonstrate your expertise by gaining recommendations from colleagues and customers.

* Connect with current and past colleagues, customers and contacts.

* Ask questions of experts.

* Answer questions in your specialist area.

* Check out people you are going to meet.

* Search for people in specific companies.

* Post job requests and find people to work with.

The power of Linkedin lies in connecting with other people, who are known as your 'connections'. You add connections by inviting people to connect to you – the process requires you to show that you already know the person you want to connect to (LinkedIn forbids direct approaches to people you do not know) – or by being invited by other people to connect to them. LinkedIn provides tools to help you find people you may know on the network.

Once connected to you, your connections are listed in your profile. They can see what are you working on when you answer the question *'What are you working on now?'* in less than 140 characters and can see your other connections (you can restrict who sees this list).

You can enhance your profile by asking your connections for 'recommendations' and by connecting to 'groups' of people with similar interests within LinkedIn.

Potential customers may check you out on LinkedIn before making direct contact. Reading what other people have said about you (your recommendations) is more powerful than reading what your company says on its corporate website. LinkedIn shows what other people say about you and highlights the company you keep.

HINT   Connect with us via LinkedIn at
http://www.linkedin.com/in/annmariehanlon and
http://www.linkedin.com/in/joannaakins.

See also

Q17   How can we use Linkedin to market our business / products / services?

Q18   How can we use LinkedIn for market research?

Q47   How do we use LinkedIn to drive traffic to our website?

Q79   How do we prevent brand damage if our employees use social networking sites?

Q82   How can we brand our business on social media sites?

Q17   How can we use LinkedIn to market our business / products / services?

People buy from other people, not from companies, especially when they are buying services.

LinkedIn is an ideal marketing tool for the solo consultant / knowledge-worker who sells their time, skills and expertise. Your profile allows you to showcase your experience and expertise, your recommendations testify to this, and your connections spread the word.

Where your aim in using LinkedIn is to market your business, or its products and services, rather than yourself, you need to add a company page.

In addition, you can create a 'group' on LinkedIn – perhaps a user interest group, or a group of key people in the same industry – which will add to your profile and connections.

There are many examples of LinkedIn generating sales for companies – for example, **Mathew Smart** at Ace Embroidery uses LinkedIn to provide updates and offers to his connections. In addition, companies have used LinkedIn to:

- Recruit key staff, basing the initial contact on the person's LinkedIn profile.
- Identify businesses for acquisition.
- Identify suppliers, based on their expertise shown in answering questions.

> **HINT**
>
> When you meet people at networking events and swap business cards, suggest you connect via LinkedIn as this provides more information about both parties and highlights any potential opportunities to work together or refer the person to another contact.

You could use LinkedIn to market your business, and its products and services, in several ways:

Tactic	How
Raising your company profile	Complete your profile, adding plenty of detail (and a photo) and asking customers and colleagues for recommendations. Use your 'Professional Headline' well. Many people just add in their job title, but this rarely properly describes the person or the company. You have a maximum of 120 characters to make your statement – for example, *Author of 'Quick Win Marketing', trainer, marketing strategist, planner & consultant at Evonomie.net in UK & Ireland* (101 characters). Then add a company page. Click on 'Companies' in the top navigation bar, 'Add a Company' and follow the instructions. Improve your profile by providing more details about your company's services and products. Recommendations from your connections about great services you have delivered (or recommendations you write about other companies) show up in your connections' updates.
Driving traffic to your website	LinkedIn can drive traffic to your website, as it appears to be searched frequently by **Google**. Ways to attract Google's attention include: ask or answer questions; update your profile (not your status) and add a company page.
Starting groups	**Plato.ie**, a business support network, uses LinkedIn to establish groups, to send messages to members and to promote its events.

See also
Q16   What is LinkedIn?
Q47   How do we use LinkedIn to drive traffic to our website?
Q79   How do we prevent brand damage if our employees use social networking sites?
Q81   What should we include in an online profile?
Q82   How can we brand our business on social media sites?

Q18 How can we use LinkedIn for market research?

You can do your own market research among your own connections in **LinkedIn** by sending them a message.

You also can use the search function on LinkedIn to identify people in different industries or industry sectors, in different jobs, companies or locations. However, unless the people you identify are already connections of yours, you cannot contact them directly. Therefore, you will need to spend time reaching out through your existing contacts to these people, seeking to connect to them, before you can contact them.

A simpler way of reaching people you don't know on LinkedIn is to use surveys conducted directly by LinkedIn, which provide:

- Access to professionals.
- Deeper insights through better targeting.
- Respondents by title, seniority, function, age, country, company size.
- Large populations of quality B2B professionals across difficult-to-reach industries, geographies and functions.

LinkedIn's 'Rules of Member Engagement' only permit surveys where:

- At least 50% of the targeted members will be eligible.
- The survey is easy to use and does not contain errors.
- The survey takes less than 15-20 minutes.
- The survey complies with market research standards.
- The survey's focus is professional rather than personal.

The way LinkedIn charges for surveys depends on:

- Number of completed surveys needed.
- Length of interview.

- Seniority level of the target audience.
- Country / location of respondents.
- Timeframe for response.

Costs vary depending on what is needed, but examples include:

- 10 minute survey to 200 respondents working in companies with a turnover of $20 million or more: charge = $150.
- 20 minute survey to 200 telecom executives about open source mobile applications: charge = $89.

The respondents are often incentivised by offering a free copy of the research or a donation to a charity on their behalf.

See also

Q10   How can we use Twitter for market research?
Q15   How can we use Facebook for market research?
Q64   How can we gather feedback from customers on new products / services?
Q70   How can we use customer surveys online?

Q19 What is Ecademy?

Similar to **LinkedIn**, **Ecademy** is a business social network founded in 1998. It sees itself as a 'wine bar rather than a conference'. Ecademy's 500,000 members are said to be more UK-based, compared to LinkedIn which has its highest concentration of members in the US.

Ecademy offers three levels of membership:

Membership level	Cost	Benefits
Member	Free.	Online profile. Feature in NetNews detailing actions or posts made on Ecademy and elsewhere on the Web.
PowerNetworker™	£10 per month (prices vary by country).	As above, plus: Advert-free pages. Better search engine optimisation with additional keywords. Discounts on events. Start and run an unlimited number of clubs. Earn commission on those who are invited and pay for membership.
BlackStar	£140.00 per month (prices vary by country).	As above, plus: Attend BlackStar-only events. Discounts on training. Other tools such as auto-responders to send messages to people seeing your profile. Higher profile in Ecademy.

See also
Q5 What is social networking?
Q20 How can we use Ecademy to market our business / products / services?

Q20   How can we use Ecademy to market our business / products / services?

Ecademy provides its users with visibility and credibility. Reputations are shared – as on **LinkedIn** – and users can connect through online networking and offline at business networking events. The main benefits are mostly for paying members and include:

Benefit	Detail
Make new contacts & find work	Have an online profile - tell others about yourself and what you do. Join clubs / business groups based around expertise and topics. Search for former colleagues. Ask for introductions through 'friends of friends'. Online networking – exchange messages with other members through the private messaging system.
Advertise your services worldwide	Post adverts in the Marketplace which are seen by other Ecademy members and visitors. Automatic search engine submission gives listings high visibility on Google and other search engines. Receive optional email alerts when another member visits your listings – for immediate follow-up.
Get business support and advice	Post and respond to blogs – ask questions, debate topics, share business advice and offer help. Join topic specific networking groups and interact with other members who have the expertise you seek. Search tools help you to find members with specific skills or knowledge.

Benefit	Detail
Meet at business networking events	Global networking – attend offline networking events. Events are run by Ecademy and approved Ecademy regional leaders. Run your own business networking events to become more visible. Get to know people face-to-face – not just online.

On the basis that 'people do business with people', Ecademy provides opportunities to connect with larger groups of people, in different locations, to place adverts, to start groups and to promote offers to contacts.

 It may be an imposition to ask people to recommend you on both LinkedIn and Ecademy. Pick the network that suits your style and needs best and concentrate on developing your profile there.

See also
Q19   What is Ecademy?
Q79   How do we prevent brand damage if our employees use social networking sites?
Q81   What should we include in an online profile?
Q82   How can we brand our business on social media sites?

Q21   What is Second Life?

Second Life is a three-dimensional virtual world available via the internet. Developed by **Linden Lab** and launched in 2003, it can be accessed through free software that allows its users, aged 18+, known as 'residents', to interact with each other.

Residents create their own 'avatar' (a cartoon-like representation of themselves) and can build, buy and trade property. Single basic accounts in Second Life are free; premium accounts (required for buying land) start at $9.95 per month. The local Second Life currency, known as Linden dollars, must be pre-purchased.

With companies becoming more aware of their carbon footprint, Second Life has developed as a space for online collaboration, virtual meetings, events and training programmes. This is ideal for sales teams in different locations discussing new product development.

However, the real business opportunity in Second Life may be saving time – for example, in concept and product testing, where you can invite a group of residents to look at an idea, comment and generate feedback.

HINT Due to the power requirements of the graphics used in Second Life, you need a reasonably up-to-date computer to run the software.

See also
Q22   What can Second Life do for our business?
Q97   How can we monetise Second Life?

Q22   What can Second Life do for our business?

Several major companies, such as Michelin, 20th Century Fox, Disney and Xerox, have established and grown significant presences in **Second Life**. They are working in Second Life in a wide variety of ways: holding meetings, conducting training, building product prototypes and simulating business situations. Other giant technology companies like Intel and IBM have saved money by holding conferences via Second Life. At the other end of the scale, PR Smith, marketing consultant and best-selling business author, sells more virtual t-shirts online in Second Life than real t-shirts offline.

Elsewhere:

- Computer brands like Dell sell PCs and Mazda has given away concept cars in Second Life.

- Sporting groups such as Adidas Reebok sell branded clothing in Second Life for users' avatars, generating real income.

- Sky News has a virtual newsroom to show behind the scenes and how the news is made.

- Educational organisations such as Harvard Law School use Second Life to hold lectures and seminars through the internet.

- Museums and tourist destinations such as the Eiffel Tower and Temple Bar in Dublin have created copies of their real life locations to encourage additional visitors.

- 20th Century Fox held a premiere for *X-Men: The Last Stand* in Second Life and University College Dublin's James Joyce Library has established the first Irish library in Second Life.

Second Life seems to have most benefit as a public relations tool. Larger organisations with dedicated marketing teams could integrate Second Life into their digital marketing strategy, while smaller companies may struggle to dedicate the time needed to establish their brand in Second Life.

See also

Organisations in Second Life: http://en.wikipedia.org/wiki/ Businesses_and_organizations_in_Second_Life.

Q23   What is YouTube?

YouTube is a video-sharing website where users can upload and share videos. YouTube is owned by **Google** and videos posted to YouTube can be viewed via the internet through websites, mobile phones, blogs and email.

It started as a website to share videos with friends and family but, over time, YouTube has grown to be a place where brands can promote themselves and smaller companies can compete with bigger organisations.

Video-sharing has many advantages for smaller businesses:

- Production costs have dropped dramatically with the advent of hand-held mini video cameras like the 'Flip'.
- The cost of adding video messages to a website has disappeared with YouTube.
- Your message can be shared with millions of people.
- It is easy to upload video to news websites.

Flip video cameras allow you to make and upload videos cheaply. From $100, with software available to download from their website, the Flip is simple to use – just flip the USB stick on the side of the camera and plug into the USB port on your computer. Your computer and your camera will start communicating and will automatically download your movies. Or, many newer digital cameras have a video mode, which can be used to record simple videos.

See also
Q24   What can YouTube do for our business?
Q52   How can we post our own videos onto our website / blog?

Q24 What can YouTube do for our business?

Businesses can use **YouTube** in many different ways:

Ways to use YouTube	Products	Services	Charities
Demonstrate how products work	✓		
Share instructions on 'how to'	✓	✓	
Upload latest adverts	✓	✓	✓
Get viewers to vote on preferred adverts	✓	✓	✓
Test market new products / services	✓	✓	✓
Demonstrate expertise	✓	✓	✓
Start campaigns	✓	✓	✓
Share latest appeals			✓
Share latest news	✓	✓	✓
Show the latest techniques	✓	✓	
Film AGMs and other meetings and share with people who could not attend	✓	✓	✓
Provide 'sneak peeks' of new products or services	✓	✓	
Highlight latest fashions	✓		
Give stories a 'human face'	✓	✓	✓
Encourage fans or supporters to upload their stories	✓	✓	✓
Upload testimonials from clients	✓	✓	
Recruit staff using a video job advert	✓	✓	✓

YouTube can save you time and money. Any situation where your company receives telephone calls or emails from people asking "How do we do this?" or "Can you tell me what this looks like?" can be turned in to a simple video and posted online. Just sign up to YouTube, free of charge, and upload videos to your company channel.

Once created and uploaded, your videos can be inserted into your company's blog or onto its website. For example, **Sugar Cubes Ponies**, which sells children's clothing, has created a video, which was uploaded to YouTube, embedded onto its website and also into its blog.

 Make sure your YouTube video is no more than two minutes long – most viewers' attention span is quite short and longer downloads can be problematic unless the viewer has a fast internet connection.

See also
Q23   What is YouTube?
Q52   How can we post our own videos onto our website / blog?
Q79   How do we prevent brand damage if our employees use social networking sites?
Q82   How can we brand our business on social media sites?

Q25 What are social bookmarking sites?

Social bookmarking websites help internet users to organise, manage and share web pages.

You can save links to sites that you might want to revisit onto bookmarking sites like **Delicious** or **StumbleUpon**, instead of creating folders on your own PC, so you can see your favourite sites from any computer.

More importantly, your bookmarks are shared with the other users of the social bookmarking site. In this way, the site reflects the most bookmarked sites, and therefore the most popular / useful sites, which makes it a great starting point when you are looking for good sites on a particular topic.

Social bookmarking sites include:

Site	Details
AddThis	A tool that allows people to bookmark and share favourite content with a button that will publish on all other bookmarking sites.
Delicious	A social bookmarking service that allows users to tag, save, manage and share web pages from a centralised source.
Digg	A place for people to discover and share content from anywhere on the web.
Reddit	A source for what's new and popular on the web. Users provide all the content and vote on what's good and what's not.
ShareThis	A tool that allows people to bookmark and share favourite content with a button that will publish on all other bookmarking sites.

Site	Details
StumbleUpon	A site that delivers high-quality pages matched to your personal preferences. These pages have been recommended by your friends or one of 8 million+ other websurfers with similar interests.
Technorati	Not exactly a bookmarking site, but the first blog search engine, Technorati has expanded to include sharing and bookmarking.

You can share your bookmarks on these sites or recommend them to others. When you save a page, it is given a 'tag'. The site uses these tags to post listings of sites that contain particular tags.

Bookmarking sites can be useful to your business because:

- Search engines index tags and the links attached to the tags – a great way of improving your ranking in search results.
- Social bookmarking sites can direct traffic to your website.
- People sharing tags may visit your website, when they find it listed under a specific tag of interest to them.

When creating your website or writing blog posts, you may wish to:

- Include 'share this' or 'add this' buttons so that your content can be bookmarked.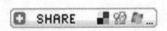
- Look at the latest tags and include these tag keywords – where relevant – into your content.

See also
Q3   What is search engine optimisation?
Q38   How do we build links to / from other websites?
Q44   How do we get higher / better search engine rankings?

Q26   What is blogging and how do we start?

Blogging is like writing a diary or journal online. The name comes from a contraction of 'weblog'. You can use a blog to share information about your business online, through a blog or a micro blog (for example, **Twitter**).

A blog article can be a sentence, paragraph or a page. It can include photos, video files (vodcasts) and sound files (podcasts). This allows you to post product reviews and demonstrations, as well as comments about your business and its products and services.

There are several free websites where you can register and choose templates to start a blog, such as **Blogger** and **WordPress.** You do not need to buy a domain name, since you can create a name that usually combines the name of your blog with the free blogging site as a suffix – for example, our blog is **business2businessmarketing.blogspot.com.** Alternatively, you can map your blog onto a domain name that you have already bought. You also can incorporate blogging software into your existing website, so that your blog is part of, and not separate from, your company website.

Blogs are a less formal customer communication than a website. They can include opinions and reviews and can influence conversations about your company. Blogs are usually open to feedback, which is a great source of soliciting customers' comments, which then (hopefully) positively influence other potential customers.

As you create blogs online, directly through the blogging website with no special PC-based software needed, you can add – or post – a new blog article from anywhere in the world.

HINT

> Several people in your organisation can be blog 'authors', which means you can share the work, perhaps each person preparing a 'post' every two weeks.

See also

Q27 How do we use blogging to market our business / products / services?

A blog can:

- Highlight your business's expertise in its industry sector.
- Share information about latest news or views.
- Provide details on how your products or services work.
- Include instructions, manuals, guides or tips.
- Give the background to PR stories from your staff's perspective.
- Provide useful information or advice.

Here's how a blog could be used in your business, for example:

Sector	How you can use a blog
Professional services	To add legal updates, or to provide checklists (for employing new staff, preparing your tax return) or views from staff – see **http://business2businessmarketing.blogspot.com**.
Website / IT	To share latest technology news, or to give examples of how clients are using your services – see **http://softwareandsupport.blogspot.com**.
Medical	To provide guidelines, information, useful links and how to get help, including patients' own stories – see **http://talk.nhs.uk/blogs/**.
Travel / holidays	To add photos, testimonials, video footage, or latest offers – see **http://www.shropshirebreakfast.co.uk/ stories.aspx?catID=19**.
Products	To show the product in action, what it can do and where it is used – see **http://www.icecreamireland.com**.
Retail	To showcase products, to capture customer comments and to share trends – see **http://sugarcubesponies.blogspot.com/**.

Sector	How you can use a blog
Design	To share news and tips about latest interior design trends and events - see **http://designagreement.blogspot.com**.

The real power of blogs for businesses include:

- **Google** likes up-to-the minute stories and sees blogs as a rich source of news. It sees your latest blog posting within a few hours – but can take weeks to index a new item on your website.

- Blogs are interactive, as readers can make comments on what you have written, although you have the power to decide whether to publish, edit or reject the comments.

- Your information can be shared with a much wider audience – potentially, new customers – as people find you online and send the link to friends or share via Twitter.

As well as creating your own blog, you can also contribute to other blogs. Both Google and **Bing** search engines include a blog search facility. If you find blogs that talk about your product or service, you can get involved in the conversation.

HINT	When blogging, whether on your own blog or commenting on a post on someone else's, consider before typing. Once you have pressed the submit key, you have very little opportunity to retract or edit what you have said, your words potentially remaining online forever as an embarrassment to you or your business.

See also

Q7   What is Twitter?
Q26   What is blogging and how do we start?
Q29   What are landing pages and how do we use them?
Q52   How can we post our own videos onto our website / blog?
Q99   How can we make money on our website / blog?

Q28   What is podcasting and how can we use it in our business?

A podcast is an audio file (usually in .MPG or .WAV format), which can be added to your website, blog, used in place of 'music on hold' on your telephone system or emailed to your customers. A podcast can be a one-off or can be a series of episodes covering specific topics – for example, 'How to implement digital marketing in your business in six easy steps'.

Before you start podcasting, you need to consider:

- What are you talking about – and why?
- Who is your audience – and why will they want to listen to you?
- Whether your podcast should be a monologue, an interview or a live production?
- What equipment do you have?

Basic podcasts can be produced using a simple digital voice recorder. More sophisticated podcasts require better quality recording equipment – for example, a Marantz recorder with a separate microphone. You can use software like **Epodcast Express** to convert your audio files for podcasting.

Before podcasting, make sure that your message meets your company's brand values. It is great if your staff can be involved too, but ensure they are aware of what the company stands for, so that they deliver the right message.

You can get training in podcasting from the appropriately-named **Podcast Training**.

Q29   What are landing pages and how do we use them?

Landing pages, also called 'lead capture' pages, are pages in your website that appear when a customer arrives to your site from a specific link on another site – for example, from the link, www.coname.com/Mayoffer or www.coname.com/Twitter.

Landing pages usually bypass your website's homepage and direct the visitor or customer to a specific page, so that you can:

- Measure the volume of traffic from specific websites, links or adverts.

- Measure the effectiveness of different adverts to see which generate greater interest and / or sales.

- Provide customised messages or offers.

The style of a landing page depends on your objectives. Do you want it to:

- Welcome specific visitors with a personalised message – for example, "Welcome, Twitter follower" for your **Twitter** followers who have clicked on a link in one of your tweets?

- Provide more information about your products or services than you provide elsewhere on your website?

- Ask potential customers to buy something – perhaps a specific model of a product or the product at a special price that includes some accessories?

- Give you some information about a particular type of customer / potential customer?

Whenever a visitor first comes to your website, you only have a few seconds to hold onto them – especially on a landing page – so don't include unnecessary information. Get your core message across quickly. You can always direct the visitor to look at other pages on your website later.

 Create landing pages if you use Twitter or LinkedIn to see how much traffic these sites direct to your website.

See also
Q7   What is Twitter?

Q30 What are content management systems and how do we use them?

Traditionally, websites were created by a technical team and, when you needed to add or delete information, you had to contact (and pay) them. However, a content management system (CMS) allows you to:

- Maintain and update your own website without technical intervention.

- Add content including text, videos, news articles, images, etc.

- View visitor statistics and make changes to your website as needed.

You need a content management system if:

- You need to update your website on a regular basis.

- You have news items to add to the home page when you're away.

- You want to add new photos or information to your website.

- You want to add / delete pages from your website.

Most good CMSs are accessible online. This means you can change your website from anywhere in the world, you don't need to be sitting at your own computer.

Some blogging tools like **Blogger** and **WordPress** are effectively CMSs. We think they're great to use as blogging tools, but harder to use to establish proper websites – although it can be done, if you're prepared to accept some lack of flexibility and functionality in return for ease of build and use.

Joomla is possibly the best known Open Source CMS. The downside is that it requires a degree of technical understanding to use; the upside is that it is free of charge.

At **Evonomie**, we use PageMasterPRO developed by **StarDigital** as our CMS, since it's easy-to-use and reliable.

See also
Q25 What are social bookmarking sites?
Q34 How can we build websites ourselves without using a web designer?
Q88 How can we monitor and measure online traffic?

Q31   What is mobile marketing and how can we use it to market our business / products / services?

Mobile marketing is marketing via mobile devices such as phone and internet. Methods of delivering mobile marketing campaigns include text messages (SMS), picture / audio messages (MMS) and mobile internet (WAP).

The main advantage of mobile marketing is that most people have mobile phones, which are always switched on and close to the owner (research suggests that people are more likely to leave home without their purse / wallet than their mobile phone).

Mobile marketing can be used in different ways, depending on the customer group and your marketing objective:

Customer group / Marketing objective	Ways to use mobile marketing
To acquire new customers	Sales promotion offers – for example, "Text this number to receive a money-off voucher".
To retain existing customers	Special offers to customers via text messages.
To provide better customer service	Information about time-critical issues, such as flight arrivals; reminders about appointments – for example, dental appointments, hair salons, etc.

Issues to be addressed before you start a mobile marketing campaign include:

- Checking the person is eligible to receive the information. It is essential to ask customers to 'opt-in' and state that they would like to receive information from you.

- Deciding how you collect the necessary mobile phone numbers. You can capture mobile telephone numbers via your website, in person or over the telephone, ensuring in each case that the customer has agreed to receive marketing or information messages from you. Alternatively, you can buy a list from a mobile marketing list broker, but do check the source of the broker's lists.

- Deciding whether or what the customer is charged for the text or picture. Deciding how to stop sending messages if the customer requests this.

- Exploring how to create compelling messages with limited text (SMS messages are limited to 160 characters).

Companies that collect individuals' mobile phone numbers or other personal information need to be registered with the **Information Commissioner** (UK) or **Data Protection Commissioner** (Ireland) and must comply with the relevant legislation to ensure they protect their customers' data.

The **Mobile Marketing Association** has chapters in the UK and Ireland, where you can network with others interested in mobile marketing.

HINT Get professional help when setting up a mobile campaign – it's easy to fall foul of the law, which will cost you time and money.

See also
Q65 How can we use SMS to contact customers / potential customers?

Q32   Why are search engine rankings important?

Just as you probably do yourself, customers and potential customers use the internet to:

- Gather information about products and services from suppliers before purchase.
- Review comments made by other customers (for example, **TripAdvisor**).
- Help them make product purchasing decisions (**eBay** rating scales).
- Add their own feedback about products and services.

They start by typing your company name, brand, product / service category or location into a search engine, such as **Google**, **Yahoo, Bing** or **Dmoz**. These search engines search across the millions of websites on the WWW based on the search terms and present back the results, in an order they believe most closely meets the searcher's needs. Most people look no further than the first page or two of search results before deciding they have all the information they need, or they search again.

Websites that are 'optimised' have a greater chance of being found in the first page or two of search results, which increases the likelihood of websurfers clicking through to them and thus the potential for sales.

A study in August 2009 by the National E-learning Laboratory on behalf of **Mulley Communications** showed that Irish users who use Google to search only pay attention to the first THREE results and that many users preferred to use Google Search to navigate to another site rather than type the site's URL in the address bar.

Sites like **Search Engine Watch** and **SearchEngineGuide** explain how search engines operate and how you can optimise your website to improve your search engine 'ranking'.

Each of the following search engines provides online advice on submitting your site to them:

- Google: http://www.google.com/addurl.
- Bing: http://www.bing.com/docs/submit.aspx.
- Yahoo: http://siteexplorer.search.yahoo.com/submit.
- Dmoz: http://www.dmoz.org/add.html.

HINT You can also submit videos, slide presentations and pictures to search engines.

See also

Q3   What is search engine optimisation?
Q44   How do we get higher / better search rankings?
Q45   How do we choose keywords / keyphrases for our website / blog?

Q33   What are the basic rules of website usability?

Website users include people with visual, hearing, physical, speech, cognitive, neurological and other disabilities. You must cater for them as well as other users. In addition, we live in a world where the population generally is aging, so it is important to consider that, as people become older, their eyesight, memory, hearing and dexterity may be reduced.

To ensure your website is universally accessible, you should consider the following:

Usability rule	Example
Simple content	Keep content simple and easy-to-read.
Clear navigation	Make sure users can navigate easily around the site and find their way back to the home page at the press of their mouse button.
Text alternatives	Offer larger print or sound files to help users to read a page.
Keyboard alternatives	Offer alternatives such as mouse-controlled pages.
Easy-to-see screen	Some colours are hard to see on screen, and customers with colour blindness may see nothing at all if you have green text on a red background! Separate foreground from background or provide alternatives; allow the user to change backgrounds.
Alternatives to images	The ALT or alternative text for an image should describe what is being shown as text readers can select and read ALT text. Be descriptive with your ALT text.
Alternatives to Flash or plug-ins	Any information in Flash or other plug-ins also should be offered in plain HTML.

Usability rule	Example
Eliminate distractions	Keep your site free from pop-ups and other distractions that can confuse visitors.

> **HINT**
>
> The World Wide Web Consortium (W3C) sets standards for web design. Good web designers will already be aware of these guidelines. Ask for examples of sites they have done and ask how they have incorporated website usability.

See also

Q1 Where do we start with digital marketing?

Q34 How can we build websites ourselves without using a web designer?

Q35 What contact information must appear at a minimum on our website / blog?

DIGITAL TOOLBOX

It's kind of fun to do the impossible.
Walt Disney

Q34   How can we build websites ourselves without using a web designer?

Websites are created using 'HTML code', which is a computer language that allows you to communicate with your computer and others (HTML stands for 'hyper text mark-up language'). Other languages, such as PHP or Java, may be used to write part of the HTML code.

A website involves:

- Building the website structure and navigation (the coding).
- Creating the design (the 'look and feel').
- Creating content (the text that appears on your web pages).
- Adding photographs, images, audio or video.
- Buying a domain name (the web address).
- Buying email services.
- Ongoing hosting.

You can build websites yourself in several ways as shown in the table on the next page, but if this all seems like too much work, you can have a professional web designer do it for you. Before signing up a web designer, check other recent sites they have developed and agree a price – negotiate!

Whichever option you select, you still need to create the content – both when you set up the website initially and on an ongoing basis, since it's important to keep your website up-to-date.

Check prices for ongoing hosting and email services, which usually require an annual payment. Note that domain names need to be renewed every one or two years.

Option	Advantages	Disadvantages
DIY – code a website yourself	There are many good books available on how to build a website from scratch, coding your own site yourself. It is free – other than the cost of the book and your time.	HTML coding can take time to learn. You may make mistakes that result in an unprofessional-looking or unreliable website. The features on your website will be limited by your ability as a coder.
DIY – using a package	Allows you to create a website without coding. Web editors include: Microsoft Expression, Macromedia Dreamweaver and Mozilla SeaMonkey.	You need to spend time learning a new software package. You still may need to involve a graphic designer. Cost.
Buy 'ready-to-go' website packages online	Cheap at the start; usually less than €100 and often include hosting, a domain name, ready-made templates and a single web page. Search for 'DIY website' to find companies providing this service.	Seems a cheaper option but may be more expensive long-term, because the domain name is often owned by the company and if you want to buy it, or to move where it is hosted, the costs can be high. Usually limited functionality, so you may have to pay dearly for a feature you particularly want.

See also

Q30 What are content management systems and how do we use them?
Q33 What are the basic rules of web usability?
Q35 What contact information must appear as a minimum on our website / blog?
Q36 What are we required to do to protect the privacy of visitors to our website / blog?

Guide to HTML: http://www.w3.org/MarkUp/Guide.

Q35   What contact information must appear as a minimum on our website / blog?

Within the European Union, websites are governed by the **EU Ecommerce Directive** (Directive 2000/31/EC on electronic commerce). The minimum information that must appear on a business website or business blog comprises:

- Your name (if you are using a trading name, you must explain this – for example, 'ABC.com is the trading name of ABC Enterprises Limited').

- The address where you trade from, which must be more than a PO Box.

- An email address.

- Company registration number, place of registration and registered office address.

- If you are licensed by any organisation or other body, details of your license.

- If you are a member of a professional body, details of the body and your membership.

- Your VAT registration number if you are registered, even if you are not selling online.

This information does not need to appear on every page, but should be easy to find. Many companies include these details on their 'About us' or 'Legal info' pages.

HINT

Emails and other electronic communications (for example, online order forms) also must include the company registration number, place of registration and registered office address.

As well as all of the information above, ecommerce websites must include clear and unambiguous prices, which state whether they are inclusive of tax and delivery costs.

See also
Q33   What are the basic rules of web usability?
Q36   What are we required to do to protect the privacy of visitors to our website / blog?

Q36   What are we required to do to protect the privacy of visitors to our website / blog?

European Parliament Directives 95/46/EC [23] and 97/66/EC [24] address the processing of personal data and the protection of privacy.

The **Office of the Data Protection Commissioner** (Ireland) sums up data responsibilities for organisations as follows:

* Obtain and process the information fairly.

* Keep it only for one or more specified and lawful purposes.

* Process it only in ways compatible with the purposes for which it was given to you initially.

* Keep it safe and secure.

* Keep it accurate and up-to-date.

* Ensure that it is adequate, relevant and not excessive.

* Retain it no longer than is necessary for the specified purpose or purposes.

* Give a copy of his / her personal data to any individual, on request.

In addition, to protect the privacy of visitors to your blog / website, you need to 'take appropriate security measures against unauthorised access to, or unauthorised alteration, disclosure or destruction of, the data, in particular where the processing involves the transmission of data over a network, and against all other unlawful forms of processing'.

Practical ways to implement these requirements include:

* One person should be appointed as 'data controller' and be responsible for collecting any data.

* Use a Secure Socket Layer (SSL) on the parts of your website where you capture and from which you retain personal data.

- Encrypt laptops that hold personal data, so that without the password the data is inaccessible.

- Train staff to make sure they do not accidentally reveal customers' personal information.

See also

Q59   Can we send an enewsletter to everyone on our database?
Q60   What rules apply to contacting people online?

Q37 Where can we get stock photos for our website / blog?

A number of websites encourage professional and amateur photographers to earn royalties or to gain recognition by posting their photos online. This makes access to great photos very affordable.

Depending on how many photos you need and how you plan to use them, there are usually several options, depending on the website:

- Some websites allow members (often membership is free) to download and use their photos free of charge within the terms of their 'Image License Agreement'. Usually this agreement prohibits free download for commercial use or re-sale.

- If you are using the photos for a large print run or to create something that you will re-sell (such as a website template, postcards, etc), you need to gain permission and pay a fee for each photo downloaded / used. Usually, the fee depends on the quality of the photo downloaded and / or your planned use of it.

- If you are looking for a large number of photos on a regular basis, some websites offer an ongoing subscription that allows you to download an agreed number of photos every month.

The cheapest photos are 'royalty-free', which means that you pay a one-off fee, based on pre-agreed usage. Otherwise, the fee is for a specific use only, with a further fee if the use is extended – for example, if you use a photo as an illustration within a book and then later decide to use it as the book cover also.

The panel on the next page shows some photo sites we use.

Increasingly, these websites are adding stock video for download and use on websites / blogs.

Website	Note
Dreamstime	Royalty-free stock photography from $0.20 each.
Fotolia	Buy royalty-free images using a credit system (1 credit = £0.75).
FreeDigitalPhotos	Photos are free for corporate and personal use. Every image is free, with an option to buy high resolution versions for use in print or graphic design.
Getty Images	Royalty-free charges based on file size.
iStockPhoto	Royalty-free stock photography, vector illustrations, stock video footage from €1.25. Buy iStock credits, then download the files you need, paying-as-you-go with credits or a customised subscription.
ShutterStock	Largest subscription-based stock photo agency in the world.
Stock.xchng	Free photos as long as you stick to the rules in the Image License Agreement. In some cases, you may need to notify the artists about using the images and give credit to them. (Now owned by istockphoto.com.)

HINT If you are creating a new website or other material, buy several photos at the same time, in the same style, to create a co-ordinated look.

See also
Q52 How can we post our own videos onto our website / blog?

Q38   How do we build links to / from other websites?

Search engines rank websites higher when there are links to and from them, believing that such links demonstrate informational value (incoming links obviously are valued more highly than outgoing).

Traditionally, companies created websites with separate links pages. But links are more useful to users if they are included (embedded) in the text, so that users can click through directly to the linked site rather having to go to another page to find the link.

Links to other websites from your site may include links to:

- Your professional associations.

- Membership organisations, such as local clubs or bodies.

- Information about your location, including a link to **Googlemaps**.

- Other pages in your website.

- Blogs that you follow.

- Book reviews relevant to your industry sector / business, with links to the books and / or reviews.

- Reviews you have written on books, travel locations or accommodation.

To get other websites to link to your website or blog is more challenging! Ways to get links include:

- Make your site easy to link to by including a 'link to us' button with a short sentence about your business and a copy of your logo so that other site owners / webmasters can download these easily.

- Add great content on your site that other sites would want to link to, such as 'how to' information or guides relevant to your sector.

- Create valid lists that people want to link to.

- Create authoritative articles that can be quoted by others.

- Submit articles to industry news sites.

- Make it easy for people to link to your articles, include 'Retweet' and 'Share this' buttons.

- Ask relevant and non-competing businesses to link to your site.

- Ask or answer questions on websites like **Yahoo! Answers**, with links to relevant resources.

HINT

Keep adding new links to your website by adding regular news items (make sure you show the source) and links to external sites.

See also

Q25   What are social bookmarking sites?
Q32   Why are search engine rankings important?
Q40   How do we get more content for our blog?
Q44   How do we get higher / better search rankings?

Q39 How do we find and get followers on Twitter?

It's not a business card competition! There are people on **Twitter** with tens of thousands of followers (they are known as 'whales') but, for most businesses, quality is a better plan than quantity. We do not recommend that you auto-follow people who follow you. Be selective, as otherwise you will waste lots of time reading tweets of no relevance to you or your business.

To find followers	To get followers
Search Use the 'advanced search' function in Twitter to find people with similar interests – for example, you can use #sailing to find people interested in sailing. **Follower search** Look at the followers of people you are following or find interesting. Using 'whois' and their name – for example, 'whois brianokane' – will show you their brief biography. Online tools – for example, Who Should I Follow – will make recommendations based on your current followers and location.	Ask a question, asking your followers to retweet (repeat) it. Reply to someone else's question and their followers will see your response. Recommend people you're following on Friday, using #ff or #followfriday. Add links to photos, as these create interest. Use a URL shortener to make sure the link fits within the 140 character Twitter limit. Add useful tweets which may be retweeted. Use #hashtags, as people will see you when searching for specific subjects.

HINT You often need to enter three tags to describe yourself in the directories. You can use different tags in different directories.

A raft of Twitter directories are now available, including: **WeFollow**, **Twellow**, **GeoFollow**, **TweetFind**, **Twitr** and **JustTweetIt**. Visit them and get listed now.

See also

Q7   What is Twitter?

Q74   How can we harness our followers on Twitter?

Q40   How do we get more content for our blog?

To stay up-to-date, blogs need content, ideally refreshed frequently and regularly. How you generate content for your blog depends on why you started your blog. For example, Kieran Murphy of Murphys Ice Cream in Dingle, Co. Kerry, Ireland has created a blog (**http://icecreamireland.com**) that talks about the ingredients used, shares recipes, provides offers to its readers and allows customers to provide feedback.

Consider these tips:

- Blog articles do not need to be *War and Peace*, they can be simply a paragraph or a few lines.

- If you receive newsletters from other sources, take one or two stories from these every week / month (making sure to add in the source of the information).

- Invite other people to become 'guest contributors'.

- Allow visitors to post content (you may wish to check their posts before publishing, in case they are spamming your blog).

- You can add feeds from **Twitter** that automatically include your latest Twitter updates. Make sure that your Twitter messages reflect your blog. If Twitter is for personal use, do not add it to your business blog!

You could also outsource the updating of your blog. For example, **Limerick County Enterprise Board**, a support agency for small businesses, outsources its blogging to **Coyote Consultancy Services Ltd** in Limerick to keep it up-to-date and useful.

HINT   Look at blogs you admire and see what content they add and how frequently.

See also

Q7   What is Twitter?

Q26   What is blogging and how do we start?

Q41   How do we buy a domain name and which domain extensions should we buy?

Many domain names have already been taken, so your first step is to decide on a potential name and to check that it's available. You can do this by entering the domain name you want in the search box on most domain registration companies' websites – for example, **Namesco**, **GoDaddy** or **IE Domain Registry** (for Irish domains only). If it's available, you can purchase it using a debit or credit card.

If the domain has been taken already by someone else, you can:

- Choose another domain name.

- Choose a different extension (see below) – often, the .com extension will be taken but the .net, .info or .biz extensions may be available.

- Backorder the domain name – this means placing an order to register the domain name when it next comes up for renewal, if the current owner, who has first rights, doesn't renew it.

- Offer to buy the domain name from the current owner. You can check who this is using the 'Who Is' facility on most domain registration companies' websites and then email the owner with an offer. Some domain registration companies will act as an intermediary for you in the purchase process – for a fee. However, check first whether the domain is live by typing the name into your browser – while some people register domain names in the hope that someone else will buy them at a premium later, few owners of live websites will be willing to sell and so you might be wasting your time making an offer.

There are restrictions on who can own some domain names. Usually, these restrictions are geographically-based – for example, .IE domains are only available to companies / residents in Ireland, while .US domains are only available to companies / residents in the USA. Other restricted domains include .EDU (for educational institutions only) and .AC.UK (for academic institutions in the UK).

If buying directly is too much hassle for you, your IT support company or web developer can buy domain names for you - usually at a cheaper rate, since many have reseller arrangements with a domain registration company.

As of June 2009, according to **Wikipedia**, there were 268 top level domain (TLD) extensions. These divide into generic TLDs, such as .COM, .NET and .EDU, and country code TLDs, one for each country, such as .UK for the UK, .IE for Ireland and .AU for Australia. Within some of the country code TLDs, there can be subdivisions – for example, .CO.UK for UK companies or .AC.UK for UK academic institutions – while other countries use just the base extension for all domains – for example, .IE applies to all Irish domains.

Because it was effectively the first widely-used TLD, most people are familiar with .COM domains, and typically start their searches for a site by looking for it with this extension. However, in the UK, .CO.UK is preferred over .COM, while in Ireland there is slow but steady growth towards use of .IE domains to reflect the 'Irishness' of locally-focused websites. The panel on the next page shows some other common domain extensions.

New domain extensions appear on a regular basis. Currently, there are discussions about developing an .ECO extension just for ecologically sound products and services!

HINT

To avoid competitors taking your traffic by using the same domain name with a different extension, it is a good idea when buying a domain to buy all available generic TLDs and any country code extensions that you may be entitled to, especially those relating to locations in which you intend to trade.

Domain extension	What it represents and is used for
.BIZ	Mainly used for small business websites where the .COM has been taken!
.EU	The European Union extension. Registration of these domain names requires registrants to be resident within the European Community or trade within this area.
.INFO	Info is used for 'resource' websites. It's the most popular extension beyond .COM, .NET and .ORG.
.MOBI	An abbreviation of 'mobile' and reserved for websites built for easy viewing on mobile devices.
.NET	An abbreviation of 'network' and most commonly used by Internet service providers or other businesses involved in the Internet.
.ORG	.ORG was one of the first top level domains that was aimed at not for profit organisations or non-commercial entities.
.TV	The country code TLD for Tuvalu, a small island nation in the Pacific Ocean. Mainly used by TV companies or those in the entertainment or media industry.

See also

List of top-level domains available:
http://en.wikipedia.org/wiki/List_of_Internet_top-level_domains.

Q42   How do we select a web designer?

Selecting a web designer is challenging, as there are now hundreds of thousands of web designers within easy reach of your computer. And, beyond the basics of usabilty and reliability, good website design is often a matter of personal taste!

It can be tempting to buy from someone offering a cheap website, but tread with caution! It is definitely not a good idea to ask your neighbour or friend to organise your website, unless this is what they do for a full-time living. A good website needs real skills, a professional approach and long-term support.

The best way to find a website designer is to:

- Start by word-of-mouth. Ask colleagues who they know and what sites these designers have developed.

- Go online and find websites you like. Contact the web owners to ask their opinions of the designers.

- Ask questions on **LinkedIn** and **Twitter** and see who is recommended and ask why they recommend them!

- Contact your local Chamber of Commerce or business club and see who is a member.

- Search online for 'website designer + your location' to see who appears in the search results.

- Check with the **Irish Internet Association** or **UK Web Design Association** for their members who may be interested.

When you have a few names, call the designers and ask for:

- Details of other websites they have completed recently.

- A meeting to talk about your proposed website.

At the meeting, you can explore whether the person / company:

- Is easy to communicate with.

- Has the technical ability (insofar as you can judge) and can provide references.

- Will be personally responsible for your website – if not, then you need to meet the person who will be.

- Can provide live demos of websites they have developed.

- Can provide case studies and references.

- Can provide other services, such as SEO.

- Is really interested in your business and helping you to achieve your goals.

Don't waste your own time and the website designers' by meeting with a dozen or more. It's better to focus on three or four and put time into choosing well between them – and it's more encouraging for a designer to put effort into a meeting with you if they have a one-in-three or one-in-four chance of winning your business, rather than feeling they have little chance because there are so many others in the competition.

At the end of the meeting, agree the next steps, which is usually for a brief to be prepared. You should take responsibility for this, so that your website includes everything you need. It's on the basis of this brief that designers will quote for the task of developing your website.

> **HINT**
>
> Some website designers contract-out part of the development work to designers in other countries (usually Eastern Europe and the Far East), so do check exactly where the work will be done and by whom.

See also
Q43   How do we brief a web designer?

Q43   How do we brief a web designer?

A web brief is usually several pages long and should address these areas:

Area	You need to consider
Website goals	What do you want the website to do for your business?
Technical requirements	Any technical needs, such as a shopping cart, blog or membership / log in system?
Timing	Are you working to a specific timescale for a launch? You need to be clear and realistic about your timescale. Web designers need between 6 and 12 weeks for a website, depending on how complex it is.
Target audiences	Who do you want to communicate with? Is your audience corporate, family, B2B, association, community or some other group?
Stakeholders	Who else is involved? Tell the designer who else is involved and what their role is – but make sure only one person is responsible for liaising with the designer.
Photos	Websites need photos! Take your own, source them online or give the web designer details of the photos that will be required. This will be an extra cost.
Words	Write down the content you want to include on your website. If writing isn't your strength, find a copywriter and ask for their help.
Updates	Who will do this? Do you want / need a content management system?
Future-proofing	Think about what you need now and might need later. Just a basic website? Or additional domain names and email forwarding? Do your future plans include a shopping cart? It's easier and cheaper to build in features when designing a website, even if they won't be used for some time, than to try to retro-fit them later.

Area	You need to consider
Promotion plan	How will people hear about your website when it's live? How does the designer create an optimised website?
Budget	Do consider what your budget is. A basic site will cost less than one with a shopping cart, or one with built-in community tools.

Web designers are not saints – good ones will suggest features that you may not have thought about but, once you have accepted their quote to deliver X, Y and Z, they're unlikely to offer to do additional unpaid work. This is why although some web designers may volunteer to prepare a brief for you, it is better if you prepare your own brief. Then ask two or three designers (no more) to quote, based on your exact requirements.

Always, always, always get written confirmation from the designer stating exactly what has been agreed.

See also
Q30   What are content management systems and how do we use them?
Q33   What are the basics of web usability?
Q34   How can we build websites ourselves without using a web designer?
Q37   Where can we get stock photos for our website / blog?
Q42   How do we select a web designer?

Q44   How do we get higher / better search rankings?

To get higher or better search rankings in search engines requires some effort! There are several factors to consider, including:

Factor	Detail
Title tags	Page titles should be descriptive; sometimes home pages are called 'home pages' – this is a waste. The page title should say something immediately descriptive about the company: 'ice cream in Ireland' or 'builders in Lichfield.'
Keywords	As the name suggests, these are important words. A cookery school might include keywords such as: learn to cook, cook classes, baking lessons, chef training.
Key phrases	Having keywords in the website is great, but a website also needs to re-use the key phrases, in proper sentences, throughout the website.
Site map	Search engines like a map to see what's connected and where.
Links	Your website needs to contain relevant links to other sites and other sites need to link to your website.
Submit to search engines	Don't forget that websites must be submitted to **Google**, **MSN** / **Bing** and **Yahoo** – they are unlikely to find you otherwise.

Adding tweets to **Twitter** or asking questions on **LinkedIn** that contain your web address can also drive traffic to your website. Google has several tools to help companies improve their keywords, for example a search-based keyword tool provides keyword ideas (see **http://www.google.com/sktool/**) and a keyword tool box (see **http://www.googlekeywordtool.com**).

If your website includes 'Flash' or 'frames' in the web design, its search rankings will always be poor, as search engines find these formats difficult to index.

See also

Q45 How do we choose keywords or keyphrases for our website / blog?

Keywords are words that businesses use on their website or blog to describe their brand, products or services and which search engines use to conduct searches. A keyphrase is a group of keywords.

If you are selling legal services aimed at company directors, your keywords may include: 'lawyer', 'legal', 'directors', and your keyphrases may be: 'legal services in Dublin for directors buying and selling companies' or 'legal help selling company'.

Most people use more than one word when searching online, which is why key phrases are important.

Also, if I am looking for a coffee machine for the office, I am likely to type into **Google**: 'Coffee machine office West Midlands'. So, if you are a supplier of coffee machines, you may want to include your location in your keywords.

Your keywords / keyphrases should be repeated in:

- Links to and from your website.
- Headings and sub-headings.
- The body text on the page.
- Any images used.
- The TITLE of your web page.
- Any testimonials from clients.

To find popular keywords, you can search:

- **Google Trends**, which analyses search results to identify the world's interest in various topics.
- **Twitter** #hashtags.

You can create good keywords by:

- Looking at keywords or keyphrases on your competitors' sites.

- Using the **Google Keyword Tool**.

- Reading the Keyword Effectiveness Index notes on **http://www.searchenginepromotionhelp.com/m/articles/sea rch-engine-optimization/kei-good-indicator.php**.

- Reading **http://en.wikipedia.org/wiki/Keyword_density**.

See also

Q3   What is search engine optimisation?
Q7   What is Twitter?
Q32   Why are search engine rankings important?
Q44   How do we get higher / better search rankings?

Q46   How do we create a social networking policy?

To ensure that your brand is not damaged online accidentally by staff, it is useful to have a social networking policy.

The policy should include:

Area	Details
Brand values	What's important to your company, what really matters.
Social networking	What this is and what it includes.
Links to your company	What is and is not acceptable.
Confidentiality	Your company's policy on client, staff, partner and supplier confidentiality.
Recommendations	Some sites request recommendations – be careful that this does not conflict with any other policies in the company.

This is an example of a social networking policy. You should adapt it for your own business and get it checked by your employment lawyer.

The ABC Company values its reputation for excellent customer service, its expertise and client confidentiality.

Social networking includes Facebook, Twitter and YouTube but, as new social networking sites appear every day, it means any website, mobile application or other tool that shares words, pictures, sound or video.

To promote the business, the ABC Company uses LinkedIn and Twitter. These posts reflect our commitment to customer service and expertise. If you engage in social networking to promote the company, you are responsible for representing the company in a professional way. Don't forget that company logos and trademarks may not be used without written consent.

If you add comments to any sites, that are not the views of the ABC Company, you need to explain that the opinions expressed are your own and do not represent the views of the company.

We respect our staff, suppliers, partners and clients. Their confidentiality is important to the ABC Company. No employee is permitted to discuss online staff, suppliers, partners and clients, the work we are doing or other client information, without prior consent.

Some sites ask for recommendations for colleagues or associates. Be aware that any recommendation you make can be used by a recruiter who could take legal action against you if it is false.

Unless managing social media is your full-time role, you should not spend more time than is necessary on these sites. Any personal networking should take place outside office hours.

If any doubt about any part of this policy, contact (name).

See also

Q47 How do we use LinkedIn to drive traffic to our website?

To get **LinkedIn** to work for you, you need to start by completing your profile in detail. There are places to add your website and blog address and it's important to create a 'landing page' on your website, a dedicated page that people from a specific website arrive at, so that you can see how much traffic arrives from LinkedIn. Update your status on a regular basis, perhaps every week or two.

Once you have completed your profile, you can:

- Ask – and answer – questions.
- Join groups and contribute to group conversations.
- Ask for – and make – recommendations.
- Create updates and include links to your website and / or blog.

As **Google** indexes questions and answers on LinkedIn, this potentially drives traffic to your website. Additionally, your network sees your recommendations, group membership and status updates and other LinkedIn members may also visit your website.

HINT Allocate 15 minutes a week to look at questions and decide whether there are opportunities for you to contribute.

See also

Q48   How do we make connections on LinkedIn with people we don't know?

LinkedIn does not encourage people to make connections with people they don't know. Connecting to someone on LinkedIn suggests that you know them well.

The only way you can invite people you don't know to connect to you is if you are a member of a group. LinkedIn contains many groups and there are bound to be several that are of interest to you – for example, there are groups for the Institute of Directors, *Dairy Foods* magazine, global energy professionals, telecom executives, farm entrepreneurs and many more.

When you want to invite someone to connect to you, LinkedIn asks you to explain how you know this person:

- Colleague – you have to select the company from your LinkedIn profile.
- Classmate – you have to choose the school from your profile.
- We've done business together – it asks at which company and you have to select from your profile.
- Friend.
- Groups & Associations – it lists the LinkedIn Groups you are a member of.
- Other – you have to add the person's email address to show that you know them.
- I don't know – in which case a new window pops up with a warning.

LinkedIn lets you invite colleagues, classmates, friends and business partners without entering their email addresses but, if someone receives an invite from you and they say that they don't know you, you'll be asked to enter an email address with each future invitation.

The power of LinkedIn is that you can ask your existing contacts to introduce you to one of their contacts. You need to select a 'Category' from a menu stating the reason which could be to discuss:

- A career opportunity.
- A consulting offer.
- A new venture.
- A job inquiry.
- An expertise request.
- A business deal.
- A reference request.
- An opportunity to get back in touch.

NB. You are limited to just 5 introductions with the free service.

Reasons why you should tread with caution when inviting people you don't know well include:

- Your new contacts will have access to ALL your connections.
- They will get access to your activity.

 HINT By contrast to LinkedIn, Ecademy encourages people to connect with those they don't know.

See also:

Q49   What are 'tagging' and 'retweets' on Twitter and how do we use them?

A tag is like an electronic highlighter pen, it makes it easier to spot a particular word or phrase on a page when you're searching later. In **Twitter**, 'hashtags' which use the symbol # are used to #tag tweets. This means you can contribute to a conversation where a specific tag is used – for example, #interior design news or #marketing update.

A retweet (RT) is where someone repeats your tweet. It's like forwarding an email to all your followers. If your tweet is 'retweeted' – for example: RT @annmariehanlon Top marketing blog see http://business2businessmarketing.blogspot.com – it means that it will be seen by anyone who follows the person who retweeted you, giving you and your tweet more exposure.

You can also retweet useful tweets yourself and share the information with your followers.

The benefit of retweeting is not only that you share information with your followers that you and they might not have had access to otherwise, but also that your retweet is seen by the original tweeter who, if they are not already following you, may decide to follow you.

HINT

It is important to thank retweeters (the people retweeting your tweets). You do it like this: '@joannaakins thanks for the RT'.

See also
Q7   What is Twitter?
Q39   How do we find and get followers on Twitter?
Q74   How can we harness our followers on Twitter?

Q50 How do we verify our Twitter account?

Anyone can open a **Twitter** account and start tweeting immediately. This has resulted in a number of fake accounts where well-known people or companies have been impersonated. To stop this, Twitter has created 'verified accounts' to prevent users impersonating others. Verified accounts feature a special seal (this does not mean that accounts without a verification seal are fake!).

An experiment at the moment, verified accounts were introduced for public officials, public agencies, famous artists, athletes and other well-known individuals at risk of impersonation. To be considered for a verified Twitter account, visit **http://twitter.com/help/verified** and fill out the feedback form to let Twitter know.

If someone is 'squatting' on your brand name, you can report this to Twitter to resolve.

HINT Check the authenticity of a Twitter account by looking at the person's website and other information they provide.

See also
Q7   What is Twitter?
Q80   How can we add credibility to our online presence?
Q82   How can we brand our business on social media sites?

Q51   How do we register our Facebook page?

Facebook introduced pages for companies in 2008 but these are only available for official representatives of the brand or organisation.

To register your Facebook company page:

- Click on 'Create a Page ...' under the Sign Up button:
- Then complete the form.
- Then, if you don't already have a Facebook account, you will have to register.

When you first register a Facebook page, its address will be www.facebook.com/pages/company/123456987 until you have 25+ fans. However, if you had a page before 31 May and had 1,000+ fans, or set up one after this date and have more than 25 fans, you can apply for a personalised page address, www.facebook.com/company. Facebook introduced the requirement for 1,000 fans to stop cyber-squatters from taking major company / brand names.

You can get fans by:

- Making requests on **Twitter** (and asking your followers to retweet your request).
- Adding a 'become a fan' button on your website or blog.
- Emailing customers and encouraging them to stay ahead with the latest news and offers by becoming a fan.

See also

Q52   How can we post our own videos onto our website / blog?

Video is an interesting medium. For some time, **Google** has been developing technology to search video as well as text.

Posting your own videos depends on the technology you are using. The easiest first step is to post the videos to **YouTube** and then download from there.

To load video to YouTube:

- Create an account (you can link to your **Twitter** or **Facebook** accounts).

- Click on 'Upload video' and select where the file is being stored.

- Then follow the instructions to load your video from YouTube into your blog or website as follows (see the table on the next page).

 See http://www.theflip.com for cheap, easy-to-use video cameras.

Tool	Steps
Blogger	Log in to your blog and go to the Dashboard. Choose Layout -> Page Elements -> Add a Gadget. Choose the Video Bar gadget. Choose a title for your video. Enter the keywords for your video.
WordPress	Visit the page for your video on YouTube. Copy the URL from the address bar. In your blog's Dashboard, go to Posts -> Add New or Pages -> Add New. Click on the Add Video button on the Upload toolbar. Click the From URL tab. Paste the YouTube video URL into the Video URL box and type a Title. Then click the Insert into Post button. The YouTube video shortcode will be inserted into your post. Publish the post.
Your own website	This depends on your website – speak to your web designer. If you use a content management system, the steps typically are: Create new page -> Add video -> Publish page.

See also

Q53   Where can we post press releases online?

Press releases will only get shared if they are newsworthy. A new contract may not be newsworthy, but a new contract to build the first solar spaceship is. Think carefully about your definition of news – more importantly, think about what readers of the media outlet you are targeting will define as 'news'.

Adding a photo (for example, posting the picture on **Flickr**) can increase the chances of your story being published.

Places to post releases online include:

Website	Details	Cost
Your own website	If you use a content management system, you can add news stories as they happen.	Free
Twitter	Tweet a story as #news with a link through to your website.	Free
Facebook	Post news items on your company page. You can include photos and videos, as well as a link through to your website.	Free
Irish Press Releases	Online press release services to Irish companies, organisations and government bodies.	Free.
Free Press Release	Submits to online websites, rather than to journalists.	Free, and other options up to $30 per release.
PR Log	Specific locations can be selected.	Free online press release service.

Website	Details	Cost
ClickPress	Provider of free tools and websites to media professionals around the world. Once news submitted to ClickPress has been approved, it is available not only to visitors to the site, but also to major web and news search engines.	Free and news releases remain in searchable archives.
Press Release Point	Public relations agency specialising in press release writing and distribution.	Free, or custom service is $25 for 1 press release.
Get2Press	Online distribution channel for presentation of press releases to media in Scandinavia, UK, Ireland, Australia, New Zealand and Singapore.	£30 for 1 press release, £270 discount card (10 releases) or annual subscription £450.
PR Web	PRWeb's distribution is global.	From $80 per release.
Pressbox	Distributes releases directly to subscribing media professionals and major new media / IT outlets.	Full distribution management charge is £150.

This is a list of some of the main places where you can submit a press release online. For a longer list, check the website, http://www.avangate.com/articles/press-release-distribution_69.htm.

See also
Q7   What is Twitter?
Q11   What is Facebook?
Q76   Should we handle our own PR online or engage an agency?

DIGITAL MARKETING

The greatest risk of all is going unnoticed.
Bill Bernbach

Q54 How do we start a digital marketing campaign?

A digital marketing campaign is just one of the promotional methods your company may use to communicate with, and attract, new customers. It should be part of your overall marketing plan.

Start by:

- Defining your target audience.
- Finding out what digital marketing methods your existing customers and / or target audience are using.
- Deciding what you want to achieve.
- Exploring whether you have enough resources and time (the amount of time needed is often overlooked or underestimated) to maintain digital marketing applications.

It can be helpful to create a list of tools, what they can be used for, what you want to use them for and who will be responsible for maintaining them.

This checklist shows how you can start your digital marketing campaign:

Tool	Use	What we will use it for	Who will maintain it
LinkedIn	Connecting with professionals and existing customers.	Answering questions and gaining expert status.	Directors and senior managers to update their own profiles every 30 days. On a rota basis, directors will ask and answer questions every 20 days.

Tool	Use	What we will use it for	Who will maintain it
Twitter	Researching.	Finding out who is talking about our company, products or services.	Set up **Tweetbeep** and get admin team to monitor and add tweets daily.
Blog	Demonstrating expert status.	Sharing examples of questions we have answered.	Once a month meeting between staff to add content which will be scheduled to appear over 30 days.

See also

Q1   Where do we start with digital marketing?
Q2   What are the advantages and disadvantages of digital marketing?
Q7   What is Twitter?
Q16   What is LinkedIn?
Q26   What is blogging and how do we start?
Q72   How do we get all our staff involved in digital marketing?

QUICK WIN MARKETING Q26 How do we develop a marketing plan?

Q55   How can we use digital applications / tools / techniques to stay in touch online with our customers?

Digital applications are valuable tools for reaching a larger audience. They also show that your company is 'moving with the times'. Digital tools are particularly useful for reaching those born into the digital era.

Use the digital tools below to promote your company and yourself, to learn about new markets, to find new customers and to interact with existing customers.

Digital tool	How to use it
Enewsletters	Use one or more of the DRIP elements as a focus to: **D**ifferentiate you – from the competition. **R**emind customers – of all your expertise and full range of products. **I**nform people – about your company, team, new products or services. **P**ersuade – to buy your product, service, take part or take up an offer.
Twitter	Tweet details of new services, reply to customers' tweets, retweet useful tweets, recommend those worthy on #followfriday.
LinkedIn	Provides an online biography of your experience and connects you to others with similar interests. Existing customers who connect to you can also see your status updates – for example, "Annmarie is holding a webinar about **Twitter** at 1pm today" – and are reminded of your services and notified of any new services.
Facebook	Setting up a **Facebook** page provides you with a dedicated area to interact with your fans.

Digital tool	How to use it
Blogs	Develop a blog. It could be an addition to your website and, depending on how you use it, could provide a fuller picture of your company, its personality and define you / your company as an expert. If required, it can be accessed by invitation only and password-protected. Blog posts can be written in advance and set to appear on specific days.
Automated dispatched emails	Depending on your ecommerce software, automated emails can notify a customer when their order has been dispatched. These can be useful for reminding customers of the benefits of ordering from your store, such as special offers, next day delivery services, gift wrap, etc.

Some other thoughts:

- If you are using digital applications, keep them up-to-date.
- Ask others how they use digital tools, to gain more insight.
- Once your digital content is out there, it is either impossible or difficult to remove it from most digital applications – be careful what you post!

See also
Q7   What is Twitter?
Q11   What is Facebook?
Q16   What is LinkedIn?
Q26   What is blogging and how do we start?
Q31   What is mobile marketing and how can we use it to market our business / products / services?
Q59   Can we send an enewsletter to everyone on our database?
Q61   How do we create an enewsletter / ezine?
Q62   Where can we find subscribers to send an enewsletter to?
Q63   How often should we make contact with our customers online?
Q68   How do we prevent our online marketing being seen as spam?
Q69   How do we make our online marketing interesting to customers / potential customers?

Q56   How can we interact with our customers online?

Interacting with customers (and potential customers) online engages them in a two-way dialogue rather than the usual one-way communication. This dialogue leads to better understanding (on both sides), trust, and thus long-term relationships.

Tools for interacting include:

- Social networks, such as **LinkedIn** and **Facebook**.
- Blogging, using applications like **WordPress** or **Blogger**.
- Micro-blogging, using micro-blogging applications like **Twitter**.
- Surveys.
- Websites.

If you already have a website, you can extend its functionality to include some of these elements – for example, by adding a weekly poll or survey, a blog, a feedback page, etc.

To get the best out of online interaction:

Do	Don't ever
Comment. Ask questions. Share information on a regular basis. Find out how often, how and what customers want to talk about or what captures their attention – you will know this from the comments under your blog updates. Create a corporate online policy for social networking and blogging. Dedicate time specifically to online interaction.	Vent your anger into the web world. Post derogatory comments. Use copyrighted material.

Don't pretend to be a customer and comment on your own reviews or blogs without identifying yourself – be genuine!

See also

Q57   How do we identify our customers using digital communications?

Offline, it can be difficult to identify your customers, especially if you sell through a wholesale / retail distribution chain. But identifying customers at a macro-level can help you to segment them, providing more directed and efficient promotional methods; at a micro-level, it allows you to interact with them as individuals.

Ways to identify customers online include:

Tactic	How to use at a macro level to identify groups of customers
Online surveys	Ask people to identify themselves by completing a survey. You may need to offer a prize or incentive to encourage them to take part in the survey.
Google Alerts	Find out where people are talking about your product online and get involved in the conversation.

Tactic	How to use at a micro level to interact with individuals as customers
Twitter	Set up a **Twitter** account. **Tweetdeck** has a function to return results for other Twitter users who use specific keywords you have chosen – for example, your company name. You can follow these people (who may follow you in return), allowing you to speak to them via updates or direct messages (DMs).
Facebook	Set up a **Facebook** page for fans to identify themselves.
SMS	Using an SMS code. For example, a sandwich bar could identify its customers by asking them to text a number from their mobile phone in order to qualify for an incentive, such as a free drink with every sandwich purchased.

Tactic	How to use at a micro level to interact with individuals as customers
Online help	Some websites include online help, where they have either a cartoon-type character (known as an 'avatar') who pops onto the screen in real-time, usually asking 'can I help you?' or a 'click here and we'll call you back' button. The immediate interaction can convert customers who are undecided about a purchase.
Your own website	Provide a 'sign up to our newsletter' functionality on your website.

See also

Q58 Should we include attachments in email campaigns?

Email campaigns are about encouraging recipients to click through to your website or ecommerce store or to take other further action – for example, to request a brochure or make an appointment. Including attachments in email campaigns may create suspicion, since recipients may think an attachment contains a virus and therefore may not open it.

Your emails also may be picked up by a spam filter – either on the recipient's computer, on their IT network, or at their internet service provider (ISP). In any of these cases, your email will not reach the intended recipient's inbox. In addition, if your own (ISP) suspects that you are spamming people, they may block your emails – while this can be sorted, it's a nuisance and potentially damaging to your online reputation.

Instead of attaching a newsletter to an email, use an enewsletter software program (there are many available) and type only an abstract – or the first few lines – of the articles you wish to write. The abstract should be sufficiently compelling to encourage readers to click through to your website to read the full article. Emailing the full text of articles to a subscriber may discourage them from reading them – hook the reader first with a few lines, then if they are interested enough to click through to your website, they'll be happy to read through the entire article.

Basing your email campaign on one or more of the DRIP elements also can help to focus a campaign and to measure its effectiveness.

DRIP Element	Example	Your communication
Differentiate	Looking for quick wins for your digital marketing? *Quick Win Digital Marketing* is a quick reference book – no need to read it page by page.	
Remind	The authors run Evonomie, a marketing consultancy that specialises in services and complex products.	
Inform	*Quick Win Digital Marketing* is ideal to dip in and out of when needed.	
Persuade	Ask your own questions and you could feature in our new book.	

See also

eMarketing eXcellence: Planning and Optimising Your Digital Marketing, Dave Chaffey, Butterworth-Heinemann (ISBN 978-0750689458).

Total Email Marketing: Maximizing Your Results from Integrated E-marketing, Dave Chaffey, Butterworth-Heinemann (ISBN 978-0750680677).

Q59 Can we send an enewsletter to everyone on our database?

No! Just because a customer or another individual is on your database does not mean that you can automatically send them enewsletters. You need their permission to do so.

There are two ways in which people can give you permission to contact them with online marketing communications:

- **Single opt-in:** A person submits their email address to a company via a form on the company's website (or otherwise) to receive ecommunications. No checks are carried out before their email address is added to the subscriber database to which the enewsletter will be sent.

- **Double opt-in:** When a person submits their email address to receive ecommunications from a company, they receive an email to that email address asking them to confirm that the address used belongs to them and that they do want to subscribe. They confirm this by clicking on a link. Thus the subscriber has chosen twice – first by asking and second by confirming – to receive the enewsletter.

Make sure you always ask people for permission to add them to your enewsletter subscriber database. When you meet people at events, ask them if they would like to receive regular enewsletters from you to the email address on their business card. You cannot assume, just that because you have been given a business card, that you have a right to send them enewsletters.

For existing customers, telephone them to ask for permission; explain who you are and what you would like to send them and how often.

Ensure an opt-out link is included on every enewsletter, so that the subscriber's name can be automatically removed from a database when an opt-out request is received.

HINT Include an 'add this email address' link to your enewsletters to ensure future enewsletters go straight into a subscriber's inbox and are not caught by their spam filter.

See also

Q36 What are we required to do to protect the privacy of visitors to our website / blog?

Q60 What rules apply to contacting people online?

Q60   What rules apply to contacting people online?

The following applications have their own terms and conditions of use:

Application	Terms of use
Twitter	You can follow any **Twitter** user. However, you will only be able to Direct Message (DM) them if they also follow you. Twitter's terms include "You must not create or submit unwanted email to any Twitter members (spam)".
LinkedIn	Seeking to connect on **LinkedIn** to someone you do not know is strictly prohibited.
Facebook	Messages can only be sent to 'members' of your group, 'fans' of your page or 'friends'. **Facebook** requires that "you will not send or otherwise post unauthorized commercial communications to users (such as spam)".
Ecademy	You can send communications to other **Ecademy** members. The rules are: When receiving a communication from a member, be courteous and listen to what they have to say; do not mass broadcast to members, except as part of a pre-agreed email thread on a particular discussion; promptly remove a member from your network list if they ask you to do so.

Best practice is to ask people to opt-in to receiving your messages.

See also
Q7   What is Twitter?
Q11   What is Facebook?
Q16   What is LinkedIn?
Q19   What is Ecademy?
Q36   What are we required to do to protect the privacy of visitors to our website / blog?
Q59   Can we send an enewsletter to everyone on our database?

Q61 How do we create an enewsletter / ezine?

An ezine is an online or electronic magazine which is usually several pages and is downloaded from a website. An enewsletter is often just one or two pages and usually emailed direct to subscribers.

Enewsletters are more than branding a plain text email to be sent to your customers. They can accommodate images and banner headings, which are more likely to excite readers into buying a product, contacting you, forwarding to a friend or colleague, etc.

Enewsletter software

You need to identify which email marketing software can accommodate your needs best, as there are many available on the market, including **ConstantContact**, **Toddle** and **Newsweaver**.

Good software should include the following elements:

Element	Details
Database	An import facility for your email addresses.
Brand	Add your company logo and corporate colour to own the space and be immediately recognisable to your customers, which adds credibility and trust.
Measure and report	This will include statistics to determine how many people: opened your email; clicked through to links in your email (and which specific links prompted interest); unsubscribed; forwarded it to a friend – and when they did so.
Test	Never send an enewsletter without testing it first, to ensure it works and looks correct in all email clients such as Gmail, Yahoo or Microsoft Outlook. A test also should detect whether the enewsletter is detected as spam and ends up in Junk email.

Enewsletter content

Include in your enewsletter only an abstract – or the first few lines – of the articles you wish to write. The abstract should be sufficiently compelling to encourage readers to click through to your website to read the full article. Emailing the full text of articles to a subscriber may discourage them from reading – hook the reader first with a few lines, then if they are interested enough to click through to your website, they'll be happy to read through the entire article.

For example, your enewsletter text might read: '*Quick Win Digital Marketing* is a book aimed at entrepreneurs wishing to find out how digital tools and techniques can help them to communicate better with customers. For more information about the book, click here [insert URL to book on publisher's ecommerce website, the URL being linked to a campaign tool such as **Google Analytics**]'.

Again, so as not to annoy your customers with too much text (and to avoid running out of things to tell them!), limit your newsletters to between four and seven items like the one above. Short and snappy gets it read!

Check your spelling – sending out an enewsletter with spelling errors looks unprofessional and can damage your brand image.

See also

Q40   How do we get more content for our blog?
Q58   Should we include attachments in email campaigns?
Q59   Can we send an enewsletter to everyone in our database?
Q69   How do we make our online marketing interesting to customers / potential customers?

Q62   Where can we find subscribers to send an enewsletter to?

The best place to start is with your current customer list. If your customers have not already opted in to receive your enewsletter, you must get each individual's permission before adding them to your enewsletter subscriber list.

New subscribers can be found by using:

Tool	How to do it
Twitter	Tweet about your enewsletter: 'Our latest enewsletter contains tips on digital marketing – sign up here [add URL]'. Do not send regular bulk tweets, otherwise people may unfollow you or your **Twitter** account may be removed as spam.
LinkedIn	Post status updates: 'Just finished our latest enewsletter, which can be found at [add URL to subscribe]'.
Your own enewsletter	Add a link to the bottom of your enewsletter: 'Please forward to a colleague who may be interested in reading our enewsletter, *Viewpoint*'.
Your email signature	Include details in your email signature: '*Viewpoint* is our regular enewsletter aimed at entrepreneurs and contains tips on digital marketing [add URL to subscribe]'.
Your own website	Include a sign up form on your website. Make sure you collect subscribers' first and last names, so you can add personalisation.
Facebook	Post on your **Facebook** Wall – for example, 'Just finished latest newsletter on *Quick Win Digital Marketing*. To view this and subscribe to our enewsletters, click here'.

Buying mailing lists can also be effective for both B2B and B2C and can be used to target, for B2B, by location, business type, size of business or, for B2C, by age, gender, location, hobbies. But make sure you read the mailing list broker's terms and conditions to determine whether the list is for single-use or multi-use. To find lists, contact the **Direct Marketing Association** (UK) or **Irish Direct Marketing Association**, or sites like **Prospect Locator** or **B2B Prospector**.

See also

Q63 How often should we make contact with our customers online?

Keeping in touch with customers is important to build and maintain relationships.

In terms of the frequency of contacting customers online:

- Too often, and your readers will eventually ignore you and may even unsubscribe from your ecommmunications.

- Not enough, and your customers will wonder whether you still exist.

Be open and honest and tell customers at the sign-up stage how often they will be sent an ecommunication (email updates, email offers or enewsletters) and provide a description of what it will be about. This way customers will be less likely to unsubscribe.

If your choice of enewsletter software permits, you may be able to allow customers to engage with your brand on a more involved level: choosing contact frequency preferences (daily, weekly, monthly), format (SMS, email, etc) and area of interest (new products, special offers, technical information, etc). This will help you to learn about your customers so that you can tailor products to their specific needs – giving you competitive advantage and helping you to build long term relationships.

Use these points as an online enewsletter frequency checklist:

- A newsletter should be sent no more than twice a month.

- Plan the dates of your newsletters and delegate a member of your team to compile it in advance so they will be ready to go on time.

- Check your spelling – sending out an enewsletter with spelling errors looks unprofessional and can damage your brand image.

- Include an unsubscribe link at the bottom of all newsletters.

- Send B2C enewsletters around pay day, which is usually at the end of the month.

> **HINT**
>
> Online stores emailing details of offers should send these randomly; otherwise, customers begin to expect the offers at specific times (for example, towards the end of a month or quarter) and may wait to receive them before placing an order at the special offer prices – and shopping elsewhere in the meantime.

See also
Q60 What rules apply to contacting people online?

www.computerweekly.com for enewsletter signup example.

Q64   How can we gather feedback from customers on new products / services?

To have a successful business, it is important to gather feedback from customers to make sure they are happy, to identify any improvements needed and find out whether there is a need for any new products / services. The easiest way to get feedback from customers is to ask them!

Many companies are afraid to ask for feedback for fear of being rejected but asking for feedback can show willingness to improve, provide customer satisfaction and remind customers you are still around (and they may even place an order when you are talking to them).

Digital tools for gathering feedback on new products and / or services include:

Feedback tool	Details
Online surveys	This is a good and cheap way of gathering feedback, although response rates may be low. An incentive may help to achieve a higher response rate, such as 'the first 50 completed surveys received will get a free USB stick'.
Pop-up questionnaires	Add an incentive, such as 'complete this questionnaire for your chance to receive X' to help achieve a higher response rate. Note: many websurfers use automatic pop-up blockers.
Second Life	See **Q21 What is Second Life?**
Rate this	**YouTube** and other websites use a star rating system to provide immediate feedback for training videos, adverts, etc.
Reviews	Ask people to write an article on your blog. This can add credibility, particularly if it's by a well-known expert.

Feedback tool	Details
Polls	Quick research to find out whether, for example, visitors like your new website.
Facebook	See **Q13 What can Facebook do for our business?**
LinkedIn	Use status updates to ask questions such as 'Annmarie Hanlon is planning a series of webinars – any suggestions for a specific topic?'.

HINT Use an even scale, say 1 to 4, for survey questions, as this encourages customers to give you better information, rather than a 1 to 5 scale, where customers may opt for the middle rating.

See also

Q65 How can we use SMS to contact customers / potential customers?

SMS stands for Short Message Service (text messages) and is mainly used to communicate directly with consumers through their mobile phones. We have not yet seen examples of SMS campaigns aimed at the B2B market!

You could use SMS to:

Use	Example
Send reminders	A doctor's surgery uses SMS to contact its customers to remind them of appointments, in order to reduce the number of missed appointments.
Inform job candidates about new vacancies	A recruitment company sends text messages to its candidates to let them know when there is a new vacancy. This is a discreet way of making contact, as many candidates are in full-time jobs and are unable to take telephone calls during working hours.
Provide alerts	Argos, a 'clicks and bricks' catalogue company, uses SMS to inform customers when items are back in stock.
Send offers	A hair salon sends text messages to its customers to let them know when they have received cancellations and that there are now appointments available. This is particularly useful around the Christmas period, when many hairdressers are fully booked.
Sales promotion	Orange uses SMS with an offer for Orange Wednesdays, which is a 2-for-1 cinema ticket offer. Orange customers text FILM to 241 and receive a text message containing a code. This is shown to the ticket desk to receive the discount (see **http://web.orange.co.uk/p/film/orange_wednesdays**).
Advertising	A motor company's television advertisements encourage viewers to send a text to a telephone number to receive immediate details about the price and specifications of a car.

Providing offers and updates by SMS can improve sales, engage customers, create viral marketing and reinforce brand products and services.

You must ensure that a STOP feature is included in an SMS campaign, to allow recipients to unsubscribe at any time.

 Seek professional advice when setting up a mobile marketing campaign. Ensure you use a reputable company, which is a member of the Mobile Marketing Association.

See also
Q31   What is mobile marketing and how can we use it to market our business / products / services?

Q66 How do we run webinars for existing / potential customers?

Webinars (seminars conducted over the web) for existing and potential customers can be about new products, 'how to' or provide other relevant information. For example, **Fortress Interlocks**, a company that designs and manufactures safety access & control systems, uses webinars to stay in touch with overseas partners and share latest product information with customers.

The steps involved in running a webinar are:

What	How
Choose webinar software	Presenter and / or user downloads the software onto their PC.
Invite delegates	If you have a list of delegates, you invite them through the webinar software. Provide time, date and webinar description and share a list of other delegates (if required).
Promote the webinar to others	Add the webinar to your website and / or blog. **Twitter** – post a tweet to your followers who may retweet (RT) to their followers. Make sure you include a link to a page on your website where people can find more information and register. Inform any membership organisations you belong to and ask them whether they will promote your webinar on their website and / or blog.
In the webinar, delegates will see	Whatever the presenter is viewing on their PC screen. This means that the presenter can show delegates how to use software, such as Twitter, etc. A list of attendees will appear down the right-hand side of each delegate's screen within a chat box.

There's a wide range of webinar software available, including **GoToMeeting** and **Nefsis**. Depending on your needs, look for these features:

- Screen sharing, so delegates can view anything the presenter has showing on their PC.

- Recording of the meeting by the presenter for posting on their website, blog, etc.

- Text chat for delegates to interact with the presenter and each other and ask questions.

To make sure that your webinar starts on time without having to deal with delegates' technical issues, include in advance details about: PC requirements and specifications (you will usually find these detailed on the webinar software website); how to ensure your audio is working; and how to check your microphone is working if using one.

See also
Q7　　What is Twitter?
Q40　　How do we get more content for our blog?

Q67 How can our team collaborate online?

Collaboration software is useful if a company has remote workers who want to stay in touch with colleagues and feel part of the team, or mobile workers who are on the road a lot of the time. It is also useful if you are working on a project with people in different locations or belonging to separate companies.

Collaboration software allows you to:

- Share tasks and keep track of what projects team members are working on.
- Live chat.
- Share documents.
- Upload and assign tasks.

The following collaboration tools are available online:

Collaboration Tool	Details	Cost
Facebook Groups	Can be used for invited members only. Select 'this group is a secret' and the group will not appear in any search engines. Useful as an intranet or for member groups.	Free.
Blogger	Set a password that only those invited can access: Log in to your account. Then Dashboards -> Settings -> Permissions -> Only People I Choose.	Free.

Collaboration Tool	Details	Cost
Google Docs	Sharing documents for editing purposes. Can be used for a timetable or a marketing action plan that everyone can see and provide updates.	Free.
Huddle	Simple, secure online workspaces containing powerful project and collaboration tools. Huddle is hosted, so there's no software to download.	Free for 1GB and 1 workspace. Other packages £10 to £125 per month.
Teambox	Includes discussion forum, chat facility (see who is online), list tasks and assign them, upload documents.	Free. Branded service from €90 per month.

Alternatively, if you have an IT support service or web designer, they may be able to create a simple and cheap bespoke intranet solution that may be more secure.

HINT If you want to collaborate privately, make sure you check all of the privacy settings on your chosen application to ensure your information is not made public.

See also
Q11   What is Facebook?
Q26   What is blogging and how do we start?

Q68   How do we prevent our online marketing being seen as spam?

Spam is unwanted junk email. Unfortunately, there is no guaranteed way to ensure your online marketing is not seen as spam. However, there are a number of things you can do to reduce the risk, including:

Tool	Prevention
Enewsletters	Add a link to your online marketing communications, saying 'Add [sender] to your safe list to ensure it arrives in your inbox'. Email management software usually ensures that emails sent using them are whitelisted with ISPs.
Twitter	Do not bombard your followers with Direct Messages. Do not repeat tweets again and again.
LinkedIn	Do not regularly send bulk emails to everyone in a group.

If your online communications are useful or have a benefit to customers / recipients (such as an offer, information, tips), they are more likely to respond and take action.

HINT Use a spam checker software program to ensure your email will not be classed as spam. Lyris ContentChecker will rate your email for its spam score.

See also
Q7   What is Twitter?
Q16   What is LinkedIn?
Q61   How do we create an enewsletter / ezine?
Q69   How do we make our online marketing interesting to customers / potential customers?

Q69   How do we make our online marketing interesting to customers / potential customers?

Online marketing communications need to be engaging and interactive. This means a two-way dialogue. Examples of interesting online communications include:

Example	Details
Competitions	Ask customers to get involved in new product / service development. In 2008, Walkers Crisps launched its Do Us A Flavour competition online and, through TV advertisements, directed entrants to its website to take part in the opportunity to design a new Walkers Crisps flavour. There were 1.1m entrants, which enabled Walkers to generate PR and to engage with its customers.
Video testimonials	Use video testimonials for others to listen to – it is always more interesting and more credible to hear an audio / video testimonial from someone rather than reading it yourself from text. Ask for comments.
Video tours	Include a tour of your offices and interview members of your team about their jobs and what they like about it – this is also useful when recruiting.
Interactive brochures	If you have a brochure, provide it online on your website, as a downloadable PDF or an interactive brochure.
Case studies	Ask customers to share their stories. Write them up as case studies to add credibility to your website. These can include photos, award winners, achievements (ask permission from customers first).
Advertisements	Use **YouTube** to upload adverts / videos online and share them virally.
Provide widgets	Help customers to share information. Add 'tweet this', 'share this', 'digg this' widgets to your website.

A widget is a small application that you can embed on a web page – for example, a currency converter or visitor number counter.

See also

Q23   What is YouTube?

Q25   What are social bookmarking sites?

Q52   How can we post our own videos onto our website / blog?

Q68   How do we prevent our online marketing being seen as spam?

Q70   How can we use customer surveys online?

Surveying customers can be a requirement of the international standard **ISO9000**. It's also good practice (and good business!) to check that your customers are happy.

You can also survey potential customers. However, this is best carried out by telephone to gather more in-depth information.

Surveys can be:

- Qualitative – to explore opinions and gather detailed feedback.

- Quantitative – to gather numbers or to rate service provision (useful when contacting larger groups or capturing a customer service score).

Examples of where you can use these techniques include:

Qualitative research	Quantitative research
Gather feedback for customer service. Find out more about a team. This information can be used to create team profiles on a website: 'What's the best thing about your job?', 'What do you like to do when you're not working at the ABC Company?'. New product development: 'If you could wave a magic wand over the ABC Company, what would you develop?'.	A scoring system for service quality: 'Out of a score of 4, please rate how well [enter company name] keeps you up-to-date with new product information'. Multiple choice: 'What promotional material do you receive, if any? Please tick all those that apply'.

Shorter surveys online are more likely to be answered. Some online survey tools tell the person the percentage of the survey completed and what's left to be done, which is a useful way to stop the customer abandoning the survey.

Useful online survey software includes **SurveyMonkey,** **ConstantContact** and **Vovici**.

HINT

After the survey is over, thank those who took part (if it is not an anonymous survey) and provide them with a synopsis of the results, if appropriate.

See also

Q10 How can we use Twitter for market research?
Q15 How can we use Facebook for market research?
Q18 How can we use LinkedIn for market research?

Q71   How do we get our blog posts to a wider audience?

The purpose of a blog can be to drive traffic to your website, or to encourage potential customers to make a purchase or to request information about your brand. To widen your audience, the first essential step is to tell people that you have a blog.

You can promote your blog offline and online. Ways to promote your blog include:

Method of promotion	Details
Promote it on Twitter	"Just posted a blog article on how to set up an online survey [add link]."
Add a link to your blog from your website	'Evonomie also writes a blog which can be read at http://business2businessmarketing.blogspot.com'.
Promote it on your Facebook page	There is nowhere to add in your blog URL but you can promote it on your Wall.
Include a link in your email signature	Joanna Akins MCIM Chartered Marketer B2B Marketing for answers to your marketing questions http://business2businessmarketing.blogspot.com
Add the URL to your business card	Also add onto your business cards details for **Twitter**, blog, website, **LinkedIn**, **Facebook** and other areas where you have an online presence.
Add details to your profiles on LinkedIn, Twitter, etc	There is an area on LinkedIn to add your website URL, blog URL and one other online presence, such as your Twitter name.

Method of promotion	Details
Encourage guest posts	Ask your clients or members of groups if they want to write a blog article to post on your blog. Ask if you can guest-post on other blogs.
Promote to groups you are a member of	Write an article and ask them to include it in their enewsletters and magazines for other members to read.
Add blog posts to Digg	**Digg** is a bookmarking site and you need to create an account for it.
Register with blog directories	Such as **BritBlog**, **Technorati** and **BlogSearchEngine** for increased online exposure.

HINT Include 'Tweet this', 'Digg this' and 'ShareThis' icons on your blog posts.

See also

Q7   What is Twitter?
Q11   What is Facebook?
Q16   What is LinkedIn?
Q25   What are social bookmarking sites?
Q26   What is blogging and how do we start?
Q47   How do we use LinkedIn to drive traffic to our website?
Q81   What should we include in an online profile?

Q72   How do we get all our staff involved in digital marketing?

Digital marketing should be an integral part of your business's operations. It is important that staff are aware of, and involved in, the process. This can be achieved by a meeting to brainstorm and to ask staff members if they have any experience in digital marketing. You may find that some write a blog, develop apps (short computer programmes for specific tasks, such as the iPhone app, *Paris 3D*, which provides a mini-map you can see on your iPhone whilst walking around Paris) or use **Twitter**.

Define what you want to achieve from digital marketing and where staff can get involved, which may be:

Your objectives	Where staff can get involved
Build relationships with your customers	By asking new customers how they heard about your company. By asking for feedback.
Promote your business	By adding items to your blog.
Gain an online presence	Via **Twitter**, **LinkedIn**.
Target a new audience	Via their **Facebook** Pages.

Social networking has opened up the possibility for companies to talk directly to their fans, followers and customers. Use this opportunity to monitor comments and take appropriate action quickly: thank 'brand ambassadors' (customers who make positive comments) and address the concerns of those making negative comments.

Note that digital marketing tools can have damaging effects on your brand and business, if employees post negative comments on social networking sites, since these conversations can be seen by anyone.

HINT

If you do not already have a social networking policy, this should be a priority.

See also

Q7   What is Twitter?

Q11   What is Facebook?

Q16   What is LinkedIn?

Q46   How do we create a social networking policy?

Q79   How do we prevent brand damage if our staff use social networking sites?

Q73   How can we work with our fans on Facebook?

Facebook offers the following features:

Facebook Feature	Description and how it is used
Profiles	A page created by a person to interact with their friends.
Pages	Used by a company or brand to engage with its fans.
Groups	An area where people have a common interest, such as The Chartered Institute of Marketing: **http://www.facebook.com/TheCIM**.
Events	Create your own event, invite people and see responses.

Using Facebook pages, your company can work with fans by posting items on its Wall, such as:

- Ask fans for feedback on blog articles, books, seminars, which can help to determine any changes needed.
- Ask fans to recommend your page to a friend.
- Use your Wall for research by asking a question for fans to answer that could help your market research: 'Where do you buy children's clothing from, and why?'.
- Put a poll on your Facebook page to find out how many of your fans have a **Twitter** account. This could identify opportunities to let others know about your tweets.
- Ask if anyone has a question on marketing (or whatever your area of expertise is) that they need to know the answer to.
- Advertise for new business by asking: 'Do you know a company that really needs our help? Let us know'.

HINT

Add your Facebook page to your email signature to let people know about it.

See also

Q74 How can we harness our followers on Twitter?

Twitter can be used in a number of ways, even though it always asks the same question: 'What are you doing?'. You have 140 characters in which to create your tweet, so keep it to the point.

Twitter can be used to:

- Share useful information found elsewhere.
- Retweet other people's tweets.
- Answer customer service questions.

Tips for using Twitter to harness followers include:

- Vary your posts – no one wants to see the same tweet repeated every few hours.

- Ask questions: 'Can anyone recommend a good designer?'. It shows that you are keen to interact and that you value other people's opinions. Some Twitter users have set up searches to pick up on keywords – in that case, a designer might respond directly to your request. **Tweetdeck** provides the facility to return search results for your keywords so you can respond quickly to those mentioning, for example, your company name.

- If someone recommends you for #followfriday (when Twitter users encourage other users to follow a particular user to boost their followers), say 'thank you' and recommend them back if you think others might like to see their updates.

- Respond to questions or comment on tweets that other tweeters are posting.

- Direct message (DM) other Twitter users for more information.

- Respond to updates by saying 'thank you' for useful information.

- Search for mentions of your company name and respond to queries and complaints.

- Provide offers: 'Special offer for Twitter users, click here for details'.

 There are tools to shorten your URL to help you to keep your tweet within 140 characters, such as: TinyURL, ShortURL, Bit.ly and Ow.ly,

See also

Q7   What is Twitter?
Q26   What is blogging and how do we start?
Q49   What are 'tagging' and 'retweets' on Twitter and how do we use them?
Q95   How can Twitter generate sales for our business?

Q75   How do we advertise online?

With all advertising, online or offline, it is essential to:

- Understand the target audience.
- Create an appropriate message.
- Get professional design help to create the ad.
- Allocate a budget for an ad campaign.

The average person sees just one in every three adverts; even then they need to see up to nine ads to remember a product or service. This means that you need to advertise at least 27 times to start gaining impact.

Options for advertising online include:

Type of Ad	Details	Advantages	Disadvantages
Pay per click	Also called cost per click and pay for clicks model, based on what you bid for each click on your ad.	Flexible pricing, can be targeted.	Some people may click through, without buying.
Pay for impressions	Pay for views ads are based on what you bid for every thousand impressions of your ad.	Raises profile, cheaper than CPC.	The wrong people may see the ad but you pay each time it appears.
Google Adwords	Ads are based on your keywords and budget.	Get onto the first page of the results as people don't look at the later pages.	Needs time, money and effort to manage and to stay at the top of the listings.

Type of Ad	Details	Advantages	Disadvantages
Facebook ads	You first need a **Facebook** account. Then go to **http://www.facebook.com /ads/create** and create the ad. Options based on pay per click or pay for impressions.	Can set budgets. Target by geography, interests and age.	People are starting to ignore ads online.
Paid for directory listings	Paid directories are seen as a resource for link-building and to gain back-links to websites.	Can get a website higher in a search engine. Useful if focused on a local area.	This may not last long and some lists are ignored by major search engines.
Banner ads	Adverts that appear on relevant web pages to promote your business. Options based on pay per click or pay for impressions.	Exposure to a larger / more targeted audience.	'Banner blindness' occurring as people ignore ads online.
Website banners	You can place banners on your own website to direct visitors to a specific page or offer.	Great for time-limited offers or to highlight news.	May distract visitors from the pages they want to see.
Using affiliates	Other people advertise and promote your website.	Can bring in customers that would not normally visit your site.	Some affiliate sites charge high commissions and high ongoing fees.

Type of Ad	Details	Advantages	Disadvantages
YouTube videos	Create your video, promotional text and keywords and pay only for results when a **YouTube** viewer clicks on your promotion.	Interesting idea and may have great viral potential.	Only available in the US at the moment!
Twitter ads	Organise paid for ads via **Twitter**, using **Twittad**, **Twittertise** or **Be A Magpie**.	Can be very targeted by geography and interests.	Some followers may stop following if a tweet contains too many adverts.

See also

Q76   Should we handle our own PR online or engage an agency?

Public Relations (PR) is about communicating with your target audience. Depending upon your company, you may have lots of people to communicate with or just a few. Whether you handle your own PR online or engage an agency depends on your budget and objectives.

To carry out your own PR online, you need resources in-house, either an existing staff member who has experience with online PR or by recruiting a new member of staff.

If you have the budget but no time, the best solution is to engage a PR agency that can achieve results in an efficient and effective manner. Because they have the experience, PR agencies can provide additional benefits, such as identifying suitable online areas quickly to post PR to reach your target audience and measuring results.

If you have time but no budget, you need to decide:

- What you want to achieve (your Specific, Measurable, Achievable, Realistic, Timed objectives).
- Who your target audience is.
- What your target audience is reading.
- Which websites your target audience uses and how.

Some staff training may be needed if you are going to manage your own PR. You need to consider:

- What's your policy for talking to journalists?
- Who can talk to journalists and will they be available out of hours?
- Do you have photos available?

PR agencies have vast experience and know what will and won't work. Even if you are considering managing your own PR, do speak to an agency to get a second opinion.

Get more information from the **Association of Online Publishers** or the **Online Publishers Association**.

 Set up Google Alerts to email you when your company name appears online anywhere new.

See also

Q53   Where can we post press releases online?

Q77   How do we select an agency to handle our PR online?

Q77 How do we select an agency to handle our PR online?

If your business is thinking about taking PR online, you may already be working with a PR company. Talk to them and find out what they can offer and how it works. If you're not using a PR agency, read **Q76 Should we handle our own PR online or engage an agency?**.

If you want a PR agency to handle your PR online, a clue to suitability is whether – and where – that PR agency appears online. Do they have a strong and widespread online presence (accounts with **Twitter, LinkedIn**, etc?). If not, they may not have the online experience you are looking for.

Use this checklist to assess potential PR agencies:

Your question	Their answer
Who are your clients for online PR?	
Have you got any online PR experience in my industry / sector?	
Do you have any case studies to show me?	
What online areas do you use to promote companies?	
Are you on Twitter? (What is your Twitter name?)	
Do you write a blog? (What is the blog's URL?)	
The web is 24/7, how do you manage out-of-hours PR requests?	
How do you measure results?	
How much will a PR campaign cost? (How will this be charged? By retainer or on time spent?)	
What results can I expect?	

Ask your shortlisted PR agencies if it would be possible to speak to some of their clients to get feedback before engaging them.

HINT	Read the small print! Some PR agencies request at least three months' notice to end a contract.

See also

Q7   What is Twitter?

Q16   What is LinkedIn?

Q26   What is blogging and how do we start?

Q76   Should we handle our own PR online or engage an agency?

BRANDING ONLINE

*Once the toothpaste is out of the tube, it is awfully hard to
get it back in.*
HR Haldeman (Presidential assistant to Richard Nixon)

Q78   How is branding online different?

A brand comprises its image, personality, uniqueness and values, as well as the products and services offered. Most brands are created to work in a face-to-face environment: buying from retailers, meeting industrial buyers or visiting professionals. Placing a computer screen between the customer and the brand creates its own challenges.

Brand power has moved away from companies toward customers. The fundamental difference is that brands can lose control online quite easily, since:

- Different computer screens can create different colours and your fabulous brand can look distorted or out of sync online with your other communications.

- Some websites only show a square version of your logo (**Twitter, Facebook**).

- People can comment on your brand and you may not be aware of their comments.

- Unhappy customers can create spoof adverts and circulate them widely.

- Very unhappy customers can set up blogs dedicated to negative remarks about your company and even encourage and capture feedback from other unhappy customers.

To manage your brand online and ensure none of these negatives happen, you need to:

- Set up **Google Alerts** to see all mentions of your company name.

- Use **Tweetdeck**, **Tweetbeep** or some other online tool to monitor the mentions of your brand on **Twitter**.

- Work with designers that are more flexible and able to adapt your brand image to meet your online needs.

- Provide staff with guidelines on your brand personality (helpful, serious, professional, etc) and ensure this is reflected online in sites like **Twitter** and **Facebook**.

- Consider your business's brand values and how these are demonstrated online. If your values are about being professional or providing excellent customer service, make sure this works well online. Respond to queries, and have a system set up so that situations are resolved before they get out of hand.

In addition, branding online puts you into a global marketplace (perhaps for the first time, your branding to date may have only been local), where anyone, anywhere can see and interact with your brand. Big potential upside – but big potential downside too!

See also
Q7   What is Twitter?
Q11   What is Facebook?
Q82   How can we brand our business on social media sites?
Q92   How can we monitor our brand or company online?

QUICK WIN MARKETING Q34 What are Google Alerts?
QUICK WIN MARKETING Q73 Do we need a brand map?

Q79　How do we prevent brand damage if our employees use social networking sites?

Employees without any guidance could use social networking sites like **Facebook**, **My Space** and **Bebo** and microblogging sites like **Twitter** to post information that could:

* Leak confidential company or client information.

* Bring your company into disrepute.

* Increase calls to your helpdesk (if they say negative things about a new product or service).

* Expose your company to legal liabilities (if they describe your competitors negatively).

* Damage your brand by contradicting your brand values or image.

Often, an IT manager's solution is simply to ban all social networking sites. But this misses out on the positive benefits of allowing staff to communicate via these networks, spreading your company brand message to their followers and friends.

So, rather than ban all social networking, it is better to have a policy in place to control it from a business point-of-view.

The key areas to address in a social networking policy are:

* Your online comments reflect your business.

* Once published, it's difficult to remove comments!

* Don't share confidential details about your company, your colleagues or clients.

* Get permission to use company logos or brand images.

* Work-time is for work; keep Facebook, MySpace, etc for home and break-time.

You need to consider how your company uses social networking. It's difficult to ban all social networking if your company uses it for its brands.

See also

Q7   What is Twitter?

Q11   What is Facebook?

Q46   How do we create a social networking policy?

Q72   How do we get all our staff involved in digital marketing?

Q80   How can we add credibility to our online presence?

Gaining credibility online via websites, blogs and social networking sites is a big issue for many businesses. Many websites do not explain who they belong to, nor do they give a human face to their owners, yet still they aim to encourage people to buy their products or services.

A team at Stanford University are exploring online credibility. Their initial research has resulted in these guidelines:

1. Make it easy to verify the accuracy of the information on your site.

2. Show that there's a real organisation behind your site.

3. Highlight the expertise in your organisation and in the content and services you provide.

4. Show that honest and trustworthy people stand behind your site.

5. Make it easy to contact you.

6. Design your site so it looks professional (or is appropriate for your purpose).

7. Make your site easy to use — and useful.

8. Update your site's content often (at least show it's been reviewed recently).

9. Use restraint with any promotional content (for example, ads, offers).

10. Avoid errors of all types, no matter how small they seem.

Smaller companies in the UK often use 0845 telephone numbers to hide their location if they are not in a large city. We believe that they can gain greater credibility by providing their actual telephone number, address and, in a perfect world, a photograph of their building or office. And publishing a mobile phone number as the only contact point for your business is a definite No, No.

See also
Q81 What should we include in an online profile?

Q81   What should we include in an online profile?

A professional online profile should include:

Item	Details
About your company	Prepare this in less than 120 characters, as this is the limit for **LinkedIn** and many other websites.
About you	A one-line statement about what your role is within the company (again, keep to the 120-character rule).
Photo	A professional photo, head-and-shoulders works best. Don't use a photo taken by friends or when you were on holiday!
Logo	Use your company logo if you can.
Links to blogs, etc.	Add links to your blog, website, **Twitter** name, etc.

Prepare your profile in Word (or your preferred wordprocessing application), spell-check it, count the characters and then copy and paste it into your online application. Save it for the next profile, updating as necessary. Alternatively, save your profile at **Retaggr**, where it can be retrieved by other online applications.

HINT

If you have a profile in Facebook that shows you having a good time with friends, it may be best to keep this profile private!

See also
Q7   What is Twitter?
Q16   What is LinkedIn?
Q80   How can we add credibility to our online presence?

Q82   How can we brand our business on social media sites?

Social media sites, like **Twitter**, **LinkedIn** and **Facebook**, for example, restrict the way a brand is presented. If you have a rectangular logo (as Evonomie does), it gets cropped into a square in Facebook and doesn't look great. So it requires some creativity to brand a business consistently, despite these restrictions.

The solution is to create two versions of your logo: one for general use and one for online in a square shape.

Branding requirements vary, depending on the site being used, as shown here:

Item	LinkedIn	Twitter	Facebook
Logo size	Only available in a Company profile. Shape: 100x60 pixels. Formats: GIF, JPG, PNG. Maximum size: 100KB.	No space for logo – can add in place of photo (see below).	Shape: Square. Formats: GIF, JPG, PNG. Maximum size: 4MB.
Background	N/A	Can incorporate your logo. Design: 1280×1024 pixels. Image: 1600×1200 pixels. Formats: GIF, JPG, PNG. Maximum size: 800KB.	N/A

Item	LinkedIn	Twitter	Facebook
Biography	Maximum: 120 characters.	Maximum: 160 characters.	Limited info can be added to 'info' but you can write as much as you like on your 'Wall'.
Photo / Picture	Formats: GIF, JPG, PNG. Maximum size: 4MB.	Can add logo in 'picture', but a photo is better. Small image is needed, ideally a crop of your face. To control how it will be cropped, upload a square picture. Formats: GIF, JPG, PNG. Maximum size: 700KB.	Can be added to photos section.

Blogging tools like **Blogger** and **WordPress** come with ready-made templates or you can create your own for greater flexibility.

HINT

Free templates are available online, but many include the creator's branding. We recommend using a designer to prepare a professional template – it will be uniquely yours. Twitter backgrounds were created for Evonomie by Gerry McLaughlin at GML. You can find other backgrounds at Twitbacks and TwitterBackgroundsGallery.

See also
Q7   What is Twitter?
Q11   What is Facebook?
Q16   What is LinkedIn?
Q80   How can we add credibility to our online presence?
Q81   What should we include in an online profile?

MANAGING, MEASURING & MAKING MONEY ONLINE

Money will come when you're doing the right thing.
Michael Philips, US economist

Q83   How do we manage Twitter and Facebook?

It's time-consuming – and you risk being off-message – to post separately to **Twitter**, **Facebook** and other social media sites. However, it is possible to add your Twitter comments to your Facebook page.

To do this, in Facebook you need to allow the tweets from Twitter:

- Go to your Facebook page.

- Click on Facebook applications.

- Choose Twitter (if it's not visible, search applications) if you want all your tweets to appear or;

- Choose Selective Twitter Status (if it's not visible, search applications) if you want to control which tweets appear.

- Add application.

- Input your Twitter user name and password, if required.

If you choose Selective Twitter Status to control which tweets are added to Facebook, just add the tag #fb at the end of each tweet in order to add your Tweets to Facebook – for example: 'To manage Twitter, I use **Tweetdeck** #fb' will appear both as a tweet on your Twitter account and on your Facebook page. The same message without the #fb will only appear as a tweet.

If you have a Facebook profile for yourself and you are also an administrator for your company's Facebook page, your tweets will appear on both your own profile page and on your company page. To avoid this (some of your tweets may be inappropriate for your company page!), open a Facebook business account. These are designed for individuals who only want to use the site to administer pages and ad campaigns. Business accounts have limited functionality and are not the same as personal accounts. However, you must choose whether to have a personal profile or a business account, as it is against Facebook's Terms of Service for individuals to have more than one account. Strictly speaking, if you already have a personal Facebook profile and then want to set up a company page / business account you must close your personal profile.

See also
Q7   What is Twitter?

Q11   What is Facebook?

Q85   How do we tweet when we're busy and manage multiple Twitter accounts?

Q86   What free software can we use to help manage Twitter?

Q84　How can we publish to several sites at the same time?

To make it easier to write once and publish to many sites at the same time, there are several tools to help:

Website	Where it will publish	Cost
Ping	Twitter, LinkedIn, Facebook, MySpace, Plurk, Tumblr, Identi.ca, BrightKite, Plaxo Pulse, LiveJournal, Bebo, Hi5, Mashable, Xanga, WordPress, Koornk, YouAre, Multiply, Yammer, Utterli, imeem, Vox, TypePad, Flickr, and StreetMavens.	Free but with adverts.
FriendFeed	Twitter, Facebook, other websites.	Free.
Postling	WordPress, Blogger, TypePad, Squarespace, Tumblr, Twitter, Facebook and Flickr.	$9 / month or $90 / year.

We use Ping as it's easy to set up publishing categories - for example, 'news' is sent to Twitter and Facebook. 'Updates' are sent to Twitter, Facebook and LinkedIn.

See also

Q7　　What is Twitter?
Q11　　What is Facebook?
Q16　　What is LinkedIn?
Q83　　How do we manage Twitter and Facebook?
Q85　　How do we tweet when we're busy and manage multiple Twitter accounts?
Q86　　What free software can we use to help manage Twitter?
Q87　　How can we manage blog posts?

Q85 How do we tweet when we're busy and manage multiple Twitter accounts?

The essence of **Twitter** is to say what you're doing at that moment. Sometimes you may be busy or planning to be out of the office, unable to tweet, but want to share forthcoming events or news relating to a later date.

In addition, some people use multiple accounts:

- In their own name.
- In their company name.
- Connected to a location.
- For other people.

There are several free online tools you can use to schedule tweets and to manage multiple accounts:

Website	Scheduling tool	Manage multiple accounts
EasyTweets	From $24 per month.	From $24 per month.
Hootsuite	Free.	Free.
PostLate	From $19.95 per month.	From $19.95 per month.
SocialOomph	Free.	$29.97 per month for SocialOomph Professional.
Twittertise	Free but basic.	N/A.

HINT The busiest tweeting days for business are Tuesday and Wednesday. Morning tweets are more likely to be re-tweeted.

If you want to promote your enewsletter, for example by sharing stories from it, rather than sending out lots of tweets one after another, use one of these tools to spread your tweets out over a few days!

See also
Q7   What is Twitter?
Q83   How do we manage Twitter and Facebook?
Q84   How can we publish to several sites at the same time?
Q86   What free software can we use to help manage Twitter?

Q86   What free software can we use to help manage Twitter?

One of the fastest growing industries online is creating applications or tools for **Twitter**. There are already over 100 applications to help you manage, or get the most out of, Twitter. They include:

Application	What it does
Mr Tweet	Makes recommendations on who to follow.
Tweetburner	URL shortening service for Twitter.
Tweet Later	Schedule Tweets over a period of time.
TweetBeep	Track who is mentioning you.
TweetGrid	Live updates for any keyword on Twitter.
Qwitter	Emails you when someone stops following you.
Twitter Grader	See how you rank on Twitter.
TwitStamp	Create a personalised Twitter badge.
Twitterfox	Firefox Twitter status Add-On.
Tweetdeck	Makes Twitter easy to use.
Twitterfon	iPhone / iPod touch application for tweeting on the move.
Twittonary	Twitter Dictionary.
Twitpic	Lets you share photos on Twitter.
TweetMeme	Finds stories from Twitter for you to retweet.

HINT   If you are not using Twitter, TweetBeep is a good way to monitor your brand.

We use **Tweetdeck** to Retweet (RT), shrink URLs, monitor mentions, add to our Facebook page and easily send Direct Messages (DM). We also use **Hootsuite** to post Tweets at a later time.

See also

Q87   How can we manage blog posts?

Time management can be a big issue when adding content online.

We have a Word document to which we add future blog posts or ideas as they arise. Then, when we have a spare 10 or 15 minutes, we prepare three or four blog posts at the same time. Our content is ready to use, all that's left is to add it to the blog tool.

In **Blogger**, at the end of the post, click on Post Options and select your preferred date and time. Click on 'Publish Post' and the post will show in your list of posts as 'scheduled'. It will then be published at the time you have chosen.

In **WordPress**, to the right of the editing screen there are various buttons, including 'Publish immediately'. To choose the date and time of publication of your post, click on 'Edit' to the right of 'Publish immediately', select your preferred date / time; the post will show in your list of posts as 'scheduled'. It will then be published at the date / time you have chosen.

You also could use **PostLater**, which costs from $19.95 per month and allows you to post to your blog, or **Twitter** or other sites at a later date.

HINT

Before going on holiday, or leaving the office for a few days, make sure you have scheduled your blog posts to appear. We usually add our posts to appear at around 9.30am on weekdays.

See also

Q7   What is Twitter?
Q26   What is blogging and how do we start?
Q84   How can we publish to several sites at the same time?

Q88   How can we monitor and measure online traffic?

To see whether your online marketing is working, you need to monitor it and measure it.

We suggest that you set SMART objectives, such as 'gain 50 new customers a month from **Facebook**'. This is easily measured, so you will know whether you have achieved your target.

Your website's content management or ecommerce system may have a facility to view and report visitor statistics. Alternatively, you can use **Google Analytics** and add the necessary code to your website.

Ways to measure traffic depend on your objectives, but you may need to know:

Item	What will this tell you?	Why?	Where can you find this out?
Products viewed / purchased	Most / least popular products.	To promote more popular products and remove less popular ones.	Your web stats package or Google Analytics.
Orders (by day, month, year)	Most / least popular days of the week, month, year (seasonal).	To add offers to increase order values at certain times. To plan web maintenance when the store is not busy.	Your web stats package or Google Analytics.
Number of visitors	Whether the site is being found and conversion rates.	To understand how your SEO is working and include SEM if necessary.	Your web stats package or Google Analytics.

Item	What will this tell you?	Why?	Where can you find this out?
Referring link	Whether your promotion is effective.	To identify which websites are good at promoting your business.	Landing pages, your web stats package or Google Analytics.
Traffic sources	Where visitors are arriving from.	To identify where your website is mentioned and most popular search engines for your business.	Landing pages, your web stats package or Google Analytics.
Keywords used to arrive at the website	Which keywords visitors are using to arrive at your site.	To improve and adapt your search engine optimisation, if necessary.	Your web stats package or Google Analytics.
Twitter effectiveness	How widely your voice is heard.	To increase or decrease tweets, to drive more traffic to your website.	**Twinfluence**; **TwitterGrader**; **TweetStats**.
Campaign statistics	How well campaigns are working.	So changes can be made where needed.	Use **Google Analytics URL Tool Builder** ad copied and pasted into links.

See also

Q30 What are content management systems and how do we use them?

StarDigital for CMS and ecommerce sites, with built-in visitor statistics.

Q89 How can we use Google Analytics to measure our web traffic?

Google Analytics is a web-based tool that gives you statistics about your website traffic and marketing effectiveness.

The **Google Analytics Tool URL Builder** can be used to measure campaigns, by inserting a campaign URL automated by Google Analytics into your enewsletters, blogs, etc. For example, you can write an email, pointed to 'Quick Win Marketing book'. You generate a tag and copy and paste the link into your website. Google Analytics shows you click-throughs from that link – and any others you have set up (up to three at any one time) – to allow you to measure the effectiveness of the campaign.

Use these Google Analytics tools to help your web traffic:

Tool	What it does
Advertising Return on Investment	Shows how many visitors you have had to your website. Identifies which keywords or AdWords are most profitable and which site content generates greatest income.
Benchmarking	See how your site compares to others in your industry sector. This information is all confidential, so it is aggregated but it provides you with a useful overview.
Goals	Set advertising and other goals and measure their effectiveness in terms of number of downloads, conversion rates etc.
Bounce rate	See whether your website entry pages have 'stickiness' (low bounce rate) or whether visitors visit only one page before leaving (high bounce rate).

See also
Q88 How can we monitor and measure online traffic?

Q90 How many visitors to our website do we need to make one sale?

Look at your visitor statistics and find out how many visits to your website were made over a period (say, a month) – ignore visits by robots.

Find out the number of orders placed on your website over this same period.

Divide one by the other – if, for example, 100 out of 1,000 visitors make a purchase on your website, your conversion rate is calculated as 100 (orders) divided by 1,000 (visitors) x 100 = 10% conversion rate.

The conversion rate may vary during seasonal times, such as Christmas or summer holidays, but, if you track it monthly, you can compare statistics on a year-on-year basis.

The conversion rate for online stores varies. For example, among our clients (you understand we can't give names), results include:

Target audience	Average sale value	Conversion rate
Business to business and consumer	€50	1.4%
Business to business and consumer	€500	1%
Consumer website	£29	4.7%
Consumer website	£50	4.4% to 5.5%

So, even though the second site has a lower conversion rate than the first, its higher average sale value would give it a higher turnover based on the same traffic.

Check this as follows:

- Site 1: 1,000 visitors at 1.4% conversion = 14 purchases @ €50 each = total sales value of €700.

- Site 2: 1,000 visitors at 1% conversion = 10 purchases at €500 each = total sales value of €5,000.

Use your visitor statistics to identify where visitors arrived from and keywords they used to arrive at your site. If you use a microsite for a specific product or service as a landing page, you may find that you get a different conversion rate from that traffic source. This information will help you to plan future online promotions.

See also
Q29   What are landing pages and how do we use them?
Q99   How can we make money on our website / blog?

Q91   How can we test our email campaigns?

After establishing that your enewsletter works well for all email clients (see **Q61**), you need to look at how effective your campaigns are. Is anyone clicking through to them?

Keep track of email campaigns that you have sent in order to compare them easily. Enewsletter marketing campaign software should be able to feedback statistics or you could add details of all your campaigns into a spreadsheet for analysis if your software does not provide comparisons between campaigns.

Test variations in your campaigns to find the best way to attract action, such as:

- Personalisation.
- Sales promotion (free delivery, free gift).
- Season.
- Day of the week.
- Time of the day.

Overleaf is a checklist to help you to manage and measure your campaigns.

HINT

Using a small section of your data, test two versions of your enewsletter subject lines to see which is most effective. This is known as split-stream testing.

Details	Example newsletter	Your newsletter 1	Your newsletter 2
Number sent	100		
Day of the week sent	Thursday		
Time of day sent	9am		
Subject line	Top tips to promote your business online		
Opens	62		
Bounces	2		
Click-throughs	10		
Forwards	0		
Unsubscribes	2		
Unopened	36		

See also

Q61 How do we create an enewsletter / ezine?

Q92 How can we monitor our brand or company online?

Online searching is the best way to determine how well-known, or well-liked, your brand is. This can be carried out in various places and using a range of tools, as shown below:

Online tool	How it can be used
Google Alerts	Set up a **Google Alert** to return chosen keywords – for example, your company name, its brands or even your own name. An email will be sent to you when your chosen keywords appear online. This will enable you to determine when and where you are being talked about, whether what's being said about you is good or bad or whether someone needs your help.
Forums	Join online forums relevant to your business to monitor whether your brand is being talked about. If you enter the conversation, ensure that you tell people exactly who you are. It is illegal in the UK to pose as a customer talking favourably about your own company's products and services or posting negative comments about competitors.
Twitter	The HP Customer Care site is rated one of the 'Ten Best Web Support Sites' by the Association of Support Professionals.
Tweetdeck	Use **Tweetdeck** to set up a column that returns your search keywords to enable you to respond quickly to anyone tweeting about your products or services – whether just to say 'thank you' or to provide advice.
Tweetbeep	Like Google Alerts for Twitter, it allows you to keep track of conversations that mention you, your products or your company. Up to 10 alerts can be organised, free of charge.

Not all online sources are spidered by robots. Always ask new customers 'how did you hear about us' to monitor unknown sources.

See also

Q7   What is Twitter?

Q78   How is branding online different?

Q79   How do we prevent brand damage if our employees use social networking sites?

Q82   How can we brand our business on social media sites?

Q93   How can we trust what we read online?

Some online sources are seen as more credible than others. The best way to check that something online is credible is to see where it is mentioned and by whom. Does the same information appear in more than one place and is it backed up by statistics (where relevant)?

Articles and press mentions in the media usually are seen as credible, because the media source and the writer usually are independent of the company / brand being written about. The **Edelman Trust** publishes a monthly barometer of the most credible sources online.

Much user-generated online content now includes a system where you can rate, review, share and forward to a friend. 'Word-of-mouse' is credible, because people can relate to it ('someone like me'). For example, **TripAdvisor** allows people to write reviews about hotels, attractions, restaurants or towns / cities they have visited. Because of abuse by competitors entering negative comments about other locations and great comments about their own hotel, TripAdvisor now monitors all comments.

Companies should use the checklist overleaf to add credibility to corporate websites and online stores, and individuals and buyers should look for the same points to determine credible sources to reduce perceived risk.

For example, **ID Security Systems** in Birmingham scan actual letters from happy clients and add them as testimonials onto its website.

Other ways of generating credibility include publishing:

- Synopses of customer surveys results.
- Polls results.
- Photos of awards events.
- Photos of your team.

Information provided	Corporate website	Online stores	Profiles
Testimonials	✓	✓	
Reviews	✓	✓	
Ratings		✓	
Stock levels	✓	✓	
Awards	✓	✓	✓
Membership logos	✓	✓	✓
Case studies	✓	✓	✓
Guarantees	✓	✓	
Return information	✓	✓	
Delivery details	✓	✓	
Complaints procedure	✓	✓	
Recommendations (on LinkedIn, etc)		✓	✓
Qualifications	✓	✓	✓

Generally, not providing enough information on your website may cause doubt.

See also
Q25   What are social bookmarking sites?
Q35   What contact information must appear as a minimum on our website / blog?
Q80   How can we add credibility to our online presence?

Q94 How can charities use Facebook to generate income?

Charities are not-for-profit organisations that use PR to increase awareness and to attract donations. Charities can use **Facebook** for recruiting new supporters and fans, fundraising, promoting events, providing information, giving support and sharing experiences.

Charities that use Facebook include the **Bat Conservation Trust**, **Cancer Research UK** and the **Irish Heart Foundation**.

Fundraising on Facebook can be encouraged by:

- Providing downloadable sponsorship forms and guidelines on how to raise money.
- Offering for sale a virtual item, such as charity cards.
- Using the page as a forum for fans to provide support for each other.
- Posting stories about how fundraisers raised money for their chosen charity.
- Saying 'thank you' when supporters raise money.
- Explaining how donations will be used.
- Posting photos of fundraising events.
- Adding videos of television adverts.
- Including a link through to an area where people can donate.

Recruiting new supporters and fans on Facebook can be encouraged by:

- Asking fundraisers to post their photos online and share with their friends.
- Asking friends to share the page.
- Adding items from the page onto **Twitter**.
- Providing useful information for sharing.

- Providing a calendar of events that others can participate in.

HINT

Charities are often very busy and maintaining a Facebook page can take time. Identify an online-savvy volunteer to act as an editor (called 'Admin' on Facebook) to help to keep the page updated.

See also

Q11   What is Facebook?
Q51   How do we register our Facebook page?
Q73   How can we work with our fans on Facebook?

Q95   How can Twitter generate sales for our business?

There are several ways to generate sales via **Twitter**.

First, promote yourself as an expert, which can be achieved by:

- Tweeting tips on your subject.
- Promoting events such as a webinar.
- Answering questions that other Twitterers ask.

This may lead people to ask you to do work for them.

You can use Twitter to look for business. If you are a website designer, you can set up a search column in **Tweetdeck** to return results for 'website designer' or, more specifically, 'can anyone recommend a good website designer'. These results provide you with an opportunity to contact the person tweeting directly and to sell them your services.

Alternatively, you can pay for advertising on Twitter, using the services below or others:

Website	How it works
TwittAd	Twitter users can post ads on their Twitter profile. Advertisers select: Categories of Twitter users. Demographics / location. Price / duration set by users.

Website	How it works
Be A Magpie	An advertiser creates their ad message and selects keywords that will help identify the best Magpie-Twitterer for the campaign. The advertiser then set their budgets, giving them complete control over the spend on a single campaign, and the number of Twitterers that can be reached for this budget is automatically calculated and displayed. Magpie identifies the most influential Magpie-Twitterers for a campaign based on the selected keywords. If there are competing advertisers for a Magpie-Twitterer, an automated online auction will commence. Bid prices are guided by the budgets previously set.

Businesses using Twitter to make sales or gain business include:

- **Oxford College of Marketing**: to recruit and communicate with students, find new tutors and share marketing education tips.

- **The Bat Conservation Trust**: to promote conservation, gain new members and promote events.

- **Hopton House Bed & Breakfast**: to showcase its location and high quality breakfasts.

- **Murphys Ice Cream**: to promote its brand, drive traffic to its blog and connect with customers.

And, according to **VentureBeat**, in mid-August 2009, **Skyblox** was the first company to use Twitter to raise funding. Skyblox's tweet said: '@skyblox twitpay $1 (of first $100,000 allocation) for First Round of Funding. Now get to work!'.

See also
Q7   What is Twitter?
Q75   How do we advertise online?
Q86   What free software can we use to help manage Twitter?

Q96   How do we set up affiliate marketing programmes?

An affiliate is someone who owns a website and advertises a merchant's products for sale on it.

If you want to set up an affiliate marketing programme for your products, this is how it works:

Area	Details
How does it work?	To implement an affiliate scheme as a merchant, you need to find an affiliate package. There are many and there is normally a fee for using them.
What's in it for the merchant?	You can increase the number of sales of your products, since they are available on many more websites than just your own.
What's in it for an affiliate?	Affiliates can sign up free and earn commission on every product purchased through their site. Commission rates vary – for example: Lovefilm.com: up to £17 per person who signs up for a free trial. Fragrancezone.co.uk: 1 to 19 sales per month = 5% commission; 20+ sales per month = 6% commission. Aquarterof.co.uk: up to 9%.
What makes a good affiliate?	A suitable affiliate is someone who owns a website (preferably one with relevant high traffic).
How does it work?	The potential affiliate goes to: Your website where they click on a link that you have added to your site to allow them to join your affiliate programme. An affiliate package provider's website (for example, **AffiliateFuture** or **Affiliate Window**) and choose merchants here.

Or you could become an affiliate for someone else (for example, Amazon) by selling their products on your website and earning commission for doing so. Check out **Commission Junction**.

HINT

Take care, as unscrupulous affiliates may engage in false and misleading advertising to get sales commissions!

See also

Q99   How can we make money on our website / blog?

Q97   How can we monetise Second Life?

Second Life has its own currency, Linden dollars, which can be exchanged within the virtual world and also extracted into the real world by converting the currency at the Lindex Exchange page and adding the money to your **PayPal** account.

On Second Life, companies sell virtual items to furnish virtual buildings and clothe virtual people. So far, the main ways to generate revenue from virtual worlds are:

Second Life used for	Example
Events and conferencing	All the major IT companies have used Second Life for conferences.
Brand promotion and PR	A well-known sports brand sold 23,000 virtual trainers.
Irish World Cup t-shirt sales	Virtual t-shirts are sold via the **Blarney Stone virtual pub** in virtual Dublin in Second Life.
Fund raising	Relay for Life, a fundraising activity of the **American Cancer Society**, also runs on Second Life. Between 2005 and 2008, it raised over 43 million Linden dollars, equivalent to over $180,000.
Tourism	Promoting the place and things to do before visitors arrive. Dublin exists in Second Life as well as in reality!
Product development	An American hotel chain built a new hotel in Second Life to see how it worked. Based on feedback from virtual visitors, it adapted the design before real-world building began.
Education	Some colleges are selling places online, as well as in person.

There are several examples of people making real money through Second Life. In 2009, the first Second Life millionaire was created: an American woman, who bought and sold virtual land online. None of the plots actually existed, but other organisations that wanted a foothold in this new world parted with their cash to establish their presence on Second Life.

See also

Q21   What is Second Life?
Q22   What can Second Life do for our business?
Q98   How do we set up a PayPal business account?

Q98   How do we set up a PayPal business account?

A **PayPal** account may be an important alternative payment option for customers buying from your website. Many people own a PayPal account (often used for buying / selling on **eBay**) and have money left sitting in their account which has not been transferred to a bank account. So make it easy for them to spend it with you!

The costs of operating a PayPal account are:

Action	Premier / Business Account
Open an account	Free.
Send money	Free.
Withdraw Funds	Free to bank accounts in the UK.
Add funds	Free.
Receive funds	1.4% +£0.20 GBP to 3.4% +£0.20 GBP.
Multiple currency transactions	Exchange rate includes a 2.5% fee (for currency conversions).

There are a number of different PayPal account types to choose from, depending upon your requirements. You need to complete a form detailing your contact information and business URL, when signing up for an account. PayPal needs your bank information and it credits your bank account with two small deposits (typically less than 20p). You need to confirm the amounts received to PayPal to finish setting up the account.

Your web developer will need to add some code to your website to add PayPal to your website as a payment option for your customers.

For other website payment options, Irish readers should visit WebPayments.ie.

See also

Q99   How can we make money on our website / blog?

Q99   How can we make money on our website / blog?

The best way to make money on your website or blog is by having an ecommerce site. However, there are many other ways for businesses to make money online.

Digital tool	How to generate money
Ecommerce website	Set up an ecommerce website to sell your products. You need a payment service provider such as **RBS WorldPay**, **PayPal**, **SagePay**, etc, which take a fee per transaction as well as charging an annual fee.
Affiliate programmes	Such as **Amazon's Associate programme.**
Business websites	Sell webinars, books, ebooks and vouchers for events.
Subscription-based websites	Sell subscriptions for information websites and online tools.
Advertising	If your website has many visitors, it can attract advertising revenues either via **Google AdSense** or direct from advertisers or via intermediaries like **DoubleClick**.
Google AdSense	A Google application that places relevant adverts on your website, according to keywords on your site. NB: you can exclude competitors!

Most B2B companies can add an element of ecommerce to their website, even if it is not their main business. For example, **Bandwidth Telecommunications**, a B2B telecoms company, uses its website to sell some telecoms systems to smaller businesses.

See also
Q98   How do we set up a PayPal business account?

Q100 What are the top 10 tips for successful digital marketing?

1. Segment your target audience. Decide who your digital marketing is targeting in terms of age, geography and profile. If you're not sure, get help.

2. Create objectives. To measure the success of a campaign, you need to set SMART objectives that are specific, measurable, achievable, realistic and timed.

3. Prepare your brand digitally. Operating online means your brand may need to adapt its logo, shorten its business description and organise some good photos.

4. Monitor mentions of your brand. If you're using digital marketing, you need to know if it's working.

5. Improve your website. Look at the keywords you're using and where your traffic comes from.

6. Make your website valuable enough to be shared. Add templates, useful tips and links so that others will retweet, share and drive traffic to your website.

7. Get professional help. There are great web designers, graphic designers and marketing professionals available to help to organise your website, brand identity, mobile and advertising campaigns.

8. Share. If you've found something useful, tell your networks. Don't forget to make sure others can share your information – include 'share this' or 'add this' buttons on your website or blog.

9. Get started. Look at the best networks to meet your objectives and generate sales for your business. Depending on your business, add presentations to **SlideShare** or video to **YouTube**.

10. Get connected to us at the links below and become a fan of ours on **Facebook**:

http://www.linkedin.com/in/annmariehanlon
http://www.linkedin.com/in/joannaakins

http://twitter.com/annmariehanlon

http://twitter.com/joannaakins

http://www.facebook.com/evonomie

Appendix: URLs of Websites Mentioned

Website	URL
AddThis	http://www.addthis.com
AddThis	http://www.addthis.com/bookmark.php
AffiliateFuture	http://www.affiliatefuture.co.uk
Affiliate Window	http://www.affiliatewindow.com
Amazon Associate programme	https://affiliate-program.amazon.co.uk
American Cancer Society	http://www.cancer.org
Annmarie Hanlon	http://www.annmariehanlon.co.uk
Association of Online Publishers	http://www.ukaop.org.uk
B&B blog	http://www.shropshirebreakfast.co.uk/blog.aspx
B2B Prospector	http://www.b2bprospector.co.uk
Bandwidth Telecommunications	https://www.bandwidth.ie
Bat Conservation Trust / Facebook	http://www.facebook.com/BatConservationTrust
Bat Conservation Trust / Twitter	http://www.twitter.com/_BCT_
Be A Magpie	http://www.be-a-magpie.com
Bebo	http://www.bebo.com
Bing	http://www.bing.com
Bing Webmaster Tools	http://www.bing.com/toolbox/webmasters
Bit.ly	http://bit.ly
Blarney Stone virtual pub / Second Life	http://slurl.com/secondlife/Dublin/81/79/25
Blendtec	http://www.willitblend.com

Website	URL
Blogger	http://www.blogger.com
BlogSearchEngine	http://www.blogsearchengine.com/submit-blog
Blogspot	http://www.blogspot.com
BrightKite	http://www.brightkite.com
BritBlog	http://www.britblog.com
Cancer Research UK	http://www.facebook.com/cancerresearchuk
ClickPress	http://www.clickpress.com
Commission Junction	http://www.cj.com
ConstantContact	http://www.constantcontact.com
Cox & Plant	http://cox-plant.co.uk/5senses/home.html
Coyote Consultancy Services Ltd	http://www.ccsl.biz
Delicious	http://www.delicious.com
Digg	http://digg.com
Direct Marketing Association	http://www.dma.org.uk
Dmoz	http://www.dmoz.org
Dreamstime	http://www.dreamstime.com
EasyTweets	https://easytweets.com
eBay	http://www.ebay.com
Ecademy	http://www.ecademy.com
Edelman Trust	http://www.edelman.com/trust
Ehow	http://www.ehow.com
Epodcast Express	http://www.industrialaudiosoftware.com/products/epodcastexpress.html
EU Ecommerce Directive	http://ec.europa.eu/internal_market/e-commerce/directive_en.htm
Evonomie	http://www.evonomie.net
Evonomie / Facebook	http://www.facebook.com/evonomie

Website	URL
Evonomie blog	http://business2businessmarketing.blogspot.com
Facebook	http://www.facebook.com
Facebook Ad guidelines	http://www.facebook.com/ad_guidelines.php
Facebook Advertising	http://www.facebook.com/advertising/?pages
Facebook Pages	http://www.facebook.com/advertising/FacebookPagesProductGuide.pdf
Facebook's Statement of Rights and Responsibilities	http://www.facebook.com/terms.php?ref=pf
Flickr	http://www.flickr.com
Flip	http://www.theflip.com
Fortress Interlocks	http://www.fortressinterlocks.com
Fotolia	http://en.fotolia.com
Free Press Release	http://www.free-press-release.com
FreeDigitalPhotos	http://www.freedigitalphotos.net
FriendFeed	http://www.friendfeed.com
GeoFollow	http://www.geofollow.com
Get2Press	http://www.get2press.co.uk
Getty Images	http://www.gettyimages.com
Gmail	http://mail.google.com
GML	http://www.gmldesignltd.com
GoDaddy	http://www.godaddy.com
Google	http://www.google.com
Google Adsense	https://www.google.com/adsense
Google AdWords	https://adwords.google.co.uk
Google Analytics	http://www.google.com/analytics
Google Analytics Tool URL Builder	http://www.google.com/support/googleanalytics/bin/answer.py?hl=en&answer=55578

Website	URL
Google Keyword Tool	http://www.googlekeywordtool.com
Google Trends	http://www.google.com/insights/search/#
Google Webmaster tools	http://www.google.com/webmasters/checklist
Googlemaps	http://maps.google.com
GoToMeeting	http://www.gotomeeting.com
Hashtags	http://www.hashtags.org
Hi5	http://www.hi5.com
HP / Twitter	http://www.twitter.com/HP_IPG
HomeSwapper	http://www.homeswapper.co.uk
HootSuite	http://www.hootsuite.com
Hopton House Bed & Breakfast / Twitter	http://www.twitter.com/HoptonHouseBnB
Huddle	http://www.huddle.net
Identi.ca	http://www.identi.ca
IE Domain Registry	http://www.domainregistry.ie
imeem	http://www.imeem.com
Information Commissioner's Office (UK)	http://www.ico.gov.uk
Interior design blog	http://designagreement.blogspot.com
Irish Direct Marketing Association	http://www.directbrand.ie/idma
Irish Heart Foundation / Facebook	http://www.facebook.com/IrishHeartFoundation
Irish Internet Association	http://www.iia.ie
Irish Press Releases	http://www.irishpressreleases.ie

Website	URL
ISO	http://www.iso.org/iso/home.htm
iStockPhoto	http://www.istockphoto.com
IT support blog	http://softwareandsupport.blogspot.com
Joomla	http://www.joomla.org
JustGiving	http://www.justgiving.com
JustTweetIt	http://www.justtweetit.com/directory
Knol	http://knol.google.com
Koornk	http://www.koornk.com
Limerick County Enterprise Board blog	http://lcoeb.blogspot.com/
Linden Lab	http://www.lindenlab.com
LinkedIn	http://www.linkedin.com
LinkedIn Terms of use	http://www.linkedin.com/static?key=user_agreement&trk=ftr_useragre
LiveJournal	http://www.livejournal.com
Lyris ContentChecker for Email	http://www.lyris.com/lunarlanding/default.aspx?source=resources-cckr
MailChimp	http://www.mailchimp.com
Mashable	http://www.mashable.com
Mathew Smart / LinkedIn	http://www.linkedin.com/in/mathewsmart
Microsoft AdCenter	https://adcenter.microsoft.com
Mobile Marketing Association	http://www.mmaglobal.com
Mr Tweet	http://www.mrtweet.com
MSN	http://www.msn.co.uk
Mulley Communications	http://www.mulley.ie/googlesearch
Multiply	http://www.multiply.com

Website	URL
Murphys Ice Cream / Twitter	http://www.twitter.com/kieranmurphy
Murphys Ice Cream blog	http://icecreamireland.com
MySpace	http://www.myspace.com
Namesco	http://www.namesco.co.uk
NearbyTweets	http://nearbytweets.com
Nefsis	http://www.nefsis.com
Newsweaver	http://www.newsweaver.com
Office of the Data Protection Commissioner (Ireland)	http://www.dataprotection.ie
Online Publishers Association	http://www.online-publishers.org
Ow.ly	http://ow.ly
Oxford College of Marketing / Twitter	http://www.twitter.com/oxcom
PayPal	http://www.paypal.com
Ping	http://www.ping.fm
Plato	http://www.plato.ie
Plaxo Pulse	http://www.plaxo.com
Plurk	http://www.plurk.com
Podcast Training	http://www.podcast-training.co.uk
Polldaddy for Twitter	http://twitter.polldaddy.com
PostLater	http://www.postlater.com
PR Log	http://www.prlog.org
PR Web	http://www.prweb.com
Press Release Point	http://pressreleasepoint.com
Pressbox	http://www.pressbox.co.uk

Website	URL
Prospect Locator	http://www.prospectlocator.co.uk
Qwitter	http://www.useqwitter.com
RBS WorldPay	http://www.rbsworldpay.com
Reddit	http://www.reddit.com
Retaggr	http://www.retaggr.com
SagePay	http://www.sagepay.com
Search Engine Optimization Made Easy	http://www.seome.org
Search Engine Guide	http://www.searchengineguide.com
SearchEngineWatch	http://www.searchenginewatch.com
Second Life	http://www.secondlife.com
Second Life blog	https://blogs.secondlife.com
ShareThis	http://sharethis.com
ShareThis button	http://sharethis.com/publishers/getbutton
ShortURL	http://www.shorturl.com
ShutterStock	http://www.shutterstock.com
SkyBlox / Twitter	http://www.twitter.com/skyblox
SlideShare	http://www.slideshare.com
SocialOomph	http://www.socialoomph.com
Sphinn.com	http://www.sphinn.com
Squarespace	http://www.squarespace.com
Squidoo	http://www.squidoo.com
Stanford Guidelines for Web Credibility	http://credibility.stanford.edu/guidelines/index.html
StarDigital	http://www.stardigital.co.uk
Stock.xchng	http://www.sxc.hu
StreetMavens	http://www.streetmavens.com
StumbleUpon	http://www.stumbleupon.com

Website	URL
Sugar Cubes Ponies	http://www.youtube.com/watch?v=CBaX66YTzh8
SurveyMonkey	http://www.surveymonkey.com
Teambox	http://www.teambox.com
Technorati	http://technorati.com
TheBigGive	http://www.thebiggive.org.uk
TinyURL	http://tinyurl.com
Toddle	http://www.toddle.com
TripAdvisor	http://www.tripadvisor.com
Tumblr	http://www.tumblr.com
TweetBeep	http://www.tweetbeep.com
Tweetburner	http://www.tweetburner.com
Tweetdeck	http://www.tweetdeck.com
TweetFind	http://www.tweetfind.com
TweetGrid	http://www.tweetgrid.com
TweetMeme	http://www.tweetmeme.com
TweetStats	http://www.tweetstats.com
Tweetzi	http://www.tweetzi.com
Twellow	http://www.twellow.com
Twibes	http://www.twibes.com
Twinfluence	http://www.twinfluence.com
Twitbacks	http://www.twitbacks.com
Twitpic	http://www.twitpic.com
Twitr	http://www.twitr.org
Twitree	http://www.twitree.com
Twitscoop	http://www.twitscoop.com
TwitStamp	http://www.twitstamp.com
Twittad	http://www.twittad.com
Twitter	http://www.twitter.com

Website	URL
Twitter Learn the lingo	http://business.twitter.com/twitter101/learning
Twitter Terms of use	http://twitter.com/tos
Twitter Backgrounds Gallery	http://twitterbackgroundsgallery.com
Twitterfon	http://www.twitterfon.com
Twitterfox	http://www.twitterfox.com
TwitterGrader	http://twitter.grader.com
Twitterment	http://www.twitterment.com
Twittertise	http://www.twittertise.com
Twittonary	http://www.twittonary.com
Twitturly	http://www.twitturly.com
TwtBiz	http://twtbiz.com
Twtbizcard	http://twtbizcard.com
Twtjobs	http://twtjobs.com
Twtpoll	http://twtpoll.com
Twtqpon	http://twtqpon.com
Twtvite	http://twtvite.com
TypePad	http://www.typepad.com
UK Web Design Association	http://www.ukwda.org
Utterli	http://www.utterli.com
Venture Beat	http://www.venturebeat.com
Vovici	http://www.vovici.com
Vox	http://www.vox.com
WebPayments.ie	http://www.webpayments.ie
WeFollow	http://www.wefollow.com
Who Should I Follow	http://www.whoshouldifollow.com
Wikipedia	http://www.wikipedia.org

Website	URL
WiredRed	http://www.wiredred.co.uk
WordPress	http://www.wordpress.com (hosted service)
WordPress	http://www.wordpress.org
World Wide Web Consortium (W3C)	http://www.w3.org
Xanga	http://www.xanga.com
Xing	http://www.xing.com
Yahoo	http://www.yahoo.com
Yahoo! Answers	http://uk.answers.yahoo.com
Yammer	http://www.yammer.com
YouAre	http://www.youare.com
YouTube	http://www.youtube.com
YouTube Ads	https://ads.youtube.com
YouTube blog	http://youtube-global.blogspot.com
YouTube Handbook	http://www.youtube.com/t/yt_handbook_home

ABOUT THE AUTHORS

ANNMARIE HANLON is a Fellow of the Chartered Institute of Marketing and a member of the Marketing Institute of Ireland. She is the Consultancy Director of Evonomie (www.evonomie.net), an independent marketing company that specialises in providing expert, impartial marketing advice to clients working in business-to-business service industries.

Over the last 20 years, she has worked with many companies to evaluate projects, carry out formative and summative evaluations, conduct research into new markets, gather primary research to establish future opportunities, develop marketing strategies, create practical action plans and deliver marketing workshops in Ireland and the UK.

A languages graduate, Annmarie has experience working in Europe and the Far East.

JOANNA AKINS is a Chartered Marketer and a member of the Chartered Institute of Marketing. She is an Associate at Evonomie and has significant experience in marketing research.

Joanna previously ran the business information library for Tarmac, a leading building materials company, delivering a research and enquiry service providing market and economic information to the Group worldwide. She was also a researcher for the corporate finance team at Grant Thornton, providing company acquisition search services involving matching buyers with companies.

She has direct experience of selling online and ran her own ecommerce store selling video games consoles and accessories worldwide.

ABOUT THE QUICK WIN SERIES

The **Quick Win** series of books – and accompanying websites – is designed for the modern, busy reader, who wants to learn enough to complete the immediate task at hand, but needs to see the information in context.

The first book / website in the series is **QUICK WIN MARKETING / www.quickwinmarketing.com**.

QUICK WIN DIGITAL MARKETING is the second in the series. Its website is **www.quickwindigitalmarketing.com**.

Titles / topics planned for 2010 include:

- QUICK WIN FINANCE
- QUICK WIN FRANCHISING
- QUICK WIN LEAN BUSINESS
- QUICK WIN SAFETY MANAGEMENT
- QUICK WIN SALES
- QUICK WIN SMALL BUSINESS.

If you are interested in contributing to the series, please contact Brian O'Kane at Oak Tree Press, 19 Rutland Street, Cork, Ireland (E: brian.okane@oaktreepress.com).

QuickWinDigitalMarketing.com

QuickWinDigitalMarketing.com is a new online resource for marketers, entrepreneurs and business managers who want to understand and use digital marketing.

A subscription site, it supports and extends the information and advice provided in this book with a growing range of questions and answers – including comments and advice from other marketers, and readers like you who have had quick wins!

Go to **www.quickwindigitalmarketing.com** today!